The Yorkshire Eskimo Omnibus Edition

(The combined works of a nonsense poet)

Ronald Town

All three hilarious poetry books in one exciting volume...

The Yorkshire Eskimo And Others

Nonsense poems
By a Yorkshire man with a weird
sense of humour

Copyright © 2018

Ronald Town

Preface

I am Yorkshire born and bred and have lived in Rotherham all my life and in the Kimberworth Park and Kimberworth for almost seventy years.

This combined volume of my three books include mainly humorous poems, the odd serious poem and humorous short stories and also memories of a childhood living on a developing estate in a simpler age when kids were safe to play in the woods and fields surrounding the estate.

Many poems and stories are based around the area in which I have lived for most my life.

I am a retired joiner and joinery lecturer and secretary at the local church which will explain the content of some of my work. I am also a train enthusiast and this is also reflected in some of my poems and short stories. I also enjoy watercolour painting.

I have never been good at sport but I have always loved archery, hence the reference to Robin Hood my early childhood hero.

Acknowledgements

Once again I would like to thank local author Jeanette Hensby, author of nine books on Rotherham and other murders, her husband Richard and especially their son in law Robin Eadon author of the Captain Thomas books, for helping me to make these books, possible and encouraging me to publish my work. I would also like to thank my good friends Ken and Celia Robins and others who allow me to use them in so many poems. They inspire me in so many ways.

Also Ray Hearne the well local known singer, song writer and poet who rekindled my love for creative writing and especially about my local area. Ray started our creative writing group at the Chislett Centre on Kimberworth a few years ago.

I would also like to thank my friend and fellow artist Jane Elizabeth Bagshaw for painting the front covers on two of my books and for being the subject of some of my poems.

Also my friends and family for listening to my poems.

Contents

The Joys of decorating

My magic train spotter's hat

My working life

My dream Holiday

Who is the very first?

The Yorkshire time traveller

Worst Christmas presents ever

My wife's won the lottery

The eternal optimist

My keys are missing

The man who never shaves

Patron Saint

Go carts on Kimberworth Park

School days

My Sporting achievements

Bungee Jumping

The knocker up of Old Kimberworth Circa 1900

David the blacksmith

Friends

I want to live forever

Transparent Daisy and invisible Dan

In a land called Sunshine

Where the Pooch tree grows

Married Bliss

The walking group

Cherry wine and a Gladstone bag

Coming Home to Yorkshire

Coming home to Yorkshire is what I dream at nights,
I'm living now in Blackpool, and service all the lights.
I live with Uncle Wally, and live on boiled ham.
He is a local celebrity and drives a Blackpool Tram.

Coming home to Yorkshire is what I want to do.
I'm living now in Chester, and working at the zoo.
I live with Aunty Betty, and live on Eccles cakes,
She works at the gallery, and discovers all the fakes.

Coming home to Yorkshire, is my greatest desire,
I'm living now in Wigan, with a taxi cab for hire.
I live with my cousin Horace, and live on Ginger Beer,
He is a famous juggler, and performs at Wigan Pier.

Coming home to Yorkshire is one of my greatest aims,
I'm living now in Liverpool and making window frames.
I live with my second cousin and live on egg and chips,
He is the local carpenter and works on sailing ships.

Coming home to Yorkshire seems impossible to me,
I'm living now in Glasgow and selling cups of tea.
I'm living with Uncle Angus and living on haggis now,
He is a small time farmer with a horse and sheep and cow.

At last I'm back in Yorkshire; it's where my future lies,
I'm living now in Kimberworth, and painting butterflies.
I'm living with my family, and all is well and good,
I'm no longer eating rubbish, but good old Yorkshire pud.

The Yorkshire Eskimo

In the land of ice and snow
Lives a Yorkshire Eskimo.
He lives with huskies all quite tame.
This is how he grew to fame.

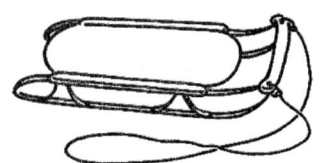

He was born in a town called Rotherham,
In a house quite near to Greasbrough dam.
William Peanut they did name him,
A name he hated and who can blame him.

He was unhappy with his lot,
Especially at times when he was hot.
But all that changed so long ago.
For his happiest time was in the snow.

He started work at fifteen, building sleds,
For a Yorkshire company in large wooden sheds.
Into his work, William put his heart and soul,
And sent his work to a warehouse at the North Pole.

He soon became the finest exponent at his game,
And overseas they spread his fame.
And finally his boss said, he'd have to let him go,
To where the Eskimos live in that land of snow.

At last he lost that stupid name,
And Billy Snowball he soon became.
He married lovely Akna of Inuit fame,
And Akna Snowball she became.

His business boomed making bespoke sleds.
Now he and Akna worked in igloo sheds.
He soon became king of them all,
That Yorkshire Eskimo, Billy Snowball.

Now Greasbrough's famous for its church and dam,
A credit indeed to fair Rotherham.
But it's most internationally famous son of all,
Is the legendary Eskimo, King Billy Snowball.

My Wardrobe

My wardrobe is full of wonder each visit brings surprise.
It's full of things long forgotten, like flares and kipper ties.
It's the story of my teenage days, a remnant of the sixties,
Of sizes belonging to a slimmer Ron, like trousers that no longer fit me.
It is a treasure trove of memories of days when quality mattered
But when trying on my sixties clothes I soon become quite shattered.

I sometimes reminisce, and clothing out I bring,
And remember those good old days, when I was a fashion King.
My velvet Jacket is long gone, along with my winkle pickers
And broad striped suits alas today are only worn by vicars.
Paisley ties are still there, along with fancy braces,
Leather belts and yellow socks, and shoes with bright red laces.

Once I chose the clothes I wore like any true Yorkshire man oughta
But now the clothes I choose are never right, too dark, too bright, too tight.
They are chosen now behind my back by my lovely wife and daughter.
For old times' sake I often wear a colourful array,
Of 70s shirts and psychedelic ties, clothes so loud they shout,
Because I can wear what I want, I'm the boss in my own house,
When my wife goes out.

My wardrobe's bursting at the seams with clothes that are too small.
But when I lose that extra stone, and a half, I'll be able to wear them all.
I'm on a diet once again and soon I'll be able to wear my treasures.
Wearing anything I want, once again, will be one of life's great pleasures.
In your dreams says my wife very much to my surprise,
Grow up Ron and chuck em out and buy some clothes your proper size.

It's the end of an era, my disappearing youth.
But she's right you know, she always is, I'll have to face the truth.
My wardrobe full of retro clothes that will never fit again,
It's all a distant memory now and it causes me such pain.
I'll have a clear out next week, and to the charity shop I'll take everything
That once made me the envy of all, the Kimberworth Park fashion King.

DIY is my game

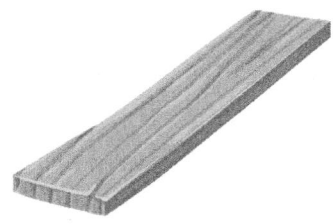

I am a DIY expert, I tell all my friends.
As for my many skills, the list it never ends.
In our new house, every job has been done.
So I keep on boasting, to my wife and to my son

"Fix me a shelf" said the love of my life.
"And do right it now if you value your life".
"Put it in the pantry two foot from the top"
"So off you go now to the local wood shop".

So I measured the shelf twice, as they tell you to do,
And wrote in my book, nine inches wide by three foot two.
So back I came from the wood yard as pleased as can be,
To find that my shelf should have been three foot three.

My wife was not pleased, I could tell from her face,
"As a DIY expert you're simply a disgrace".
So back to the shop embarrassed I went,
Life would be simpler if we lived in a tent.

Back to the pantry with my new piece of wood,
My wife will be happy and life will be good.
My wife came to see, expecting good news,
To find I had no bearers, no plugs and no screws

Back to the shop with a flea in my ear,
I wish I was in the pub, with a pie and some beer
The jobs finally done, I'm now walking tall,
But the following day it fell of the wall.

The moral is this, is don't boast of your skill,

And when jobs need doing pretend to be ill.
Be well prepared before jobs come around,
And bury all your tools in a hole in the ground.

Pockets

Tradesmen have trousers with plenty of pockets
They put rulers in some, and in others put sockets.
If you're ever in need of a nail or a screw,
A biro or string, or a packet of lockets.
Just ask a tradesman with plenty of pockets.

In them are kept screwdrivers, and sandpaper too
Things you can read, and things you can chew
On November the fifth, if you run out of rockets,
Just send for a tradesman with some in his pockets.

Some work on a farm, and just out of habit,
Out of their trousers they'll pull out a rabbit.
And if they're quite posh, and wear Harris Tweed,
In one of their pockets, you'll find carrot seed.

When working in winter, with solder and fittings,
In a plumber's pockets, are warm woollen mittens.
When buying his equipment, he's given a docket.
And guess where he puts it, straight into his pocket.

When you start work and a tradesman become,
You'll need special trousers, so go tell your mum.
If your taste in clothes, friends try to mock it.
They're jealous of your trousers, with more than one pocket.

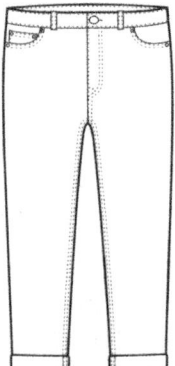 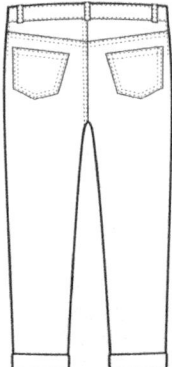

My Long Working Life

Some people are lucky, in their vocation in life,
Getting the wrong job's like getting the wrong wife.
Nine hours a day, dragging around a tool bag.
Then going home to a nagging wife is also a drag.

Nine hours a day, five days a week,
Hating every minute, and your future is bleak.
Fifty years of graft, and nothing good to mention,
Feeling your age, and a pittance of a pension.

Where did it all go wrong, you often stop to think,
Fifty years down a coal mine or at the kitchen sink.
Please let it be over, when will it all end?
Hating your job is like being without a friend.

But some good can come in everyone's life,
Like the company of good friends, children, husband or wife.
Make best of the evenings, weekends and holidays too,
Let retirement change your lifestyle and bring joy to you.

Learn to knit, crochet, or paint, or make a garden seat,
Walk in the country, with friends is something you can't beat.
And join them in the pub, for pie and peas now and then.
And then home to take your tablets, and Horlicks, and in bed by ten.

A Church Secretary's Break

August is here and it's time for a rest,
I've worked hard all year, and I've done our best.
No more activities or meetings, craftwork and such,
I can do our own thing now, thank you very much.

Maybe a holiday in the country, or days by the sea,
No more early mornings, or agendas for me.
A walk in the woods, with friends, on a warm summer's day,
This is life at its best and nothing to pay

Or catching up with the housework, or decorating chores,
Or working in the garden, with midge bites and sores.
But it's a change from the routine; we have all year long,
Its sausages on the barbeque, and singing a song.

A glass of real ale, on a warm summer's night,
Flowers and fruit in the garden, O what a sight.
Good news to all, for Augusts' here once again,
But don't get your hopes up, it's starting to rain.

Ken the Viking

Viking Ken tall and hearty,
Liked nothing better, than a party.
He only had, one constant fear,
Where to get, the perfect beer.

He'd got no barley, hops or oats,
His only hope lay, in his father's boats,.
So he sailed one day, at the crack of dawn.
And sailed into some, far distant morn.

He landed in Ireland, in a bleak summer's fog,
And found a brewery, near an ancient peat bog.
Its ales were dark, and strong and sweet,
And blew the socks, right off his feet.

It's not for me, these dark Irish Ales.
I'll cross the sea tomorrow, and go into Wales.
He entered his boat, feeling quite ill,
And at half past three, he landed in Rhyl.

There's only one cure, he said looking quite pale,
It's a flagon of the finest, strong Welsh light ale.
In Bronwyn's ale house, much to his delight,
He drank the amber nectar, far into the night.

In his search for the best, this drink was quite near,
But alas even this, was not his one perfect beer.
He left Wales that day, and on his face was a frown.
And ended his journey, in fair Rotherham town.

He entered a tavern saying "can I get a meal here",
You certainly can sir, said owner the fair Celia.
During his meal, romance was soon budding,
Partly because, of her grand Yorkshire pudding.

She suggested a drink, like any good landlady oughta,

And at the very first sip, it made his mouth water.
I've ended my search, he said, with a cheer,
I've found me a wife, who brews the perfect beer.

You may think this is rubbish, but believe me it's true,
And if you just listen now, I'll prove it to you.
Centuries have passed, since that search for real ale,
And I'm nearing the end, of my Viking Ken tale.

History repeats itself, I've heard now and then,
For his Viking's ancestors, are also called Celia and Ken.
What a coincidence, this is, you cannot beat that.
And in senior moments, Ken wears a horned hat.

Hats of all Shapes and Sizes

So here' a bit of history, for all that it is worth,
Our ancestors all wore caps, up here in the north.
They wore flat caps like huge dustbin lids
They were once the height of fashion with men and their kids

The fifties kids wore cowboy hats, and Davy Crocket hats to boot,
And pretend to be Hopalong Cassidy, and with cap guns did shoot.
Only grownups then wore proper hats, but their kids they never would,
They'd rather play in the local woods and live like Robin Hood

At the age of eleven, I wore a school cap, but only for one day,
And on my way home from school, I threw that cap away.
With my short trousers, and blazer, I looked a pretty sight,
But wear a cap with a neb on, to me just didn't seem right.

Balaclavas were all the rage, with the kids down our street,
They kept you warm in winter, in frost, snow or sleet.
In the seventies and eighties, caps went out of fashion,
I had a red bobble hat, knitted for me, which I hated with a passion.

Baseball caps were popular, in the north, just a few years ago,
And all the kids wore them, come sun, rain or snow.
I disliked them wholeheartedly, and that's speaking blunt,
Baseball caps were fine with me, but they wore them back to front.

Fleece hats are now all the rage, and I've got a few of these,
They protect your head all day long, against the winter breeze.
You can get gloves, and scarf to match, which to me is sound,
You can buy them in almost any shop, for just about five pound.

I wear mine in the garage, and it really is a must,
It keeps my head as warm as toast, and protects it from saw dust.
Caps were always worn in the north, though southerners may frown,
We've never been keen on bowler hats, as men from London Town.

The Byrley Road Merry Men
(Pronounced Burly Road)
Byrley Road is on Kimberworth Park Rotherham

The Byrley Road merry men,
Were out and about, by half past ten.
Down Kimi Park Road, in bright procession,
With bow and arrow, our proud possession.
Sometimes we'd walk, and sometimes we ran,
So I'll tell you now, how it all began.

It was one of those life changing events.
That moment when your life changes for the good.
Mine happened in nineteen fifty six,
After watching, the first episode of Robin Hood.

Now Errol Flynn were great, and Richard Todd were good,

But to me and me mates,
Richard Greene, were the real Robin Hood.
He could shoot, an arrow straight and true,
In greenwood, with a bow, made of good English yew.

We watched him throughout the winter,
And archery was now in our blood.
And when summer holidays came at last,
We were straight into Scholes wood.

Woods were just on the doorstep,
And like all other kids under ten.
The first thing we did in Scholes coppice,
Was to make ourselves a new den.

There was plenty of wood to make bows
And arrows, with corn flake box flights.
We'd chase around woods all day,
Fighting for poor people's rights.

We'd choose a big tree for a target,
And practice all day long.
You could stay out till it were dark in the fifties,
Without doing anything wrong.

Life was fun in those days.
In summers, when it never rained.
And health and safety, hadn't been invented,
In a life before blame and claim.

Mum and dad never saw us,
From early morning till night.
From Scholes, to Wentworth and Elsecar,
Our summers were happy and bright.

I still have a yearning to fire arrows,
And I still have a go now and then.
But the happiest days, were in Scholes coppice,
With me mates, me bow and me den.

For we were, the Byrley Road merry men.
Ron, Ron, Les, Dave, Barry, Dennis, Glenn and Ken

Writing Letters

Writing letters is a skill that is disappearing, as each year ends.
We were brought up to write letters, to family and to friends.
We'd get a brand new writing pad, the best that we could buy,
We'd use our favourite fountain pen, in days long gone by.
But the ballpoint became more popular, and it's still the same today,
With pen and paper ready, we'd think of what to say.

In our best hand writing, we'd write dear Malcolm, Jane of friend,
And write our letter neatly, with yours sincerely at the end.
I usually had more than one attempt, before the final draft,
If you read what I had put, you surely would have laughed.
At last our letter was complete, with envelope and stamp,
We'd write the rest another day, for fear of writer's cramp.

I can't remember the last time, I wrote a proper letter,
I stopped doing these years ago, just as I was getting better.
So how do we keep in contact, with friends and family?
My brother uses Facebook, but Email that's for me.
Many people use texts today, those modern day trend setters,
I think I'll fill my fountain pen and write some proper letters.

My Brilliant Friend Ken

If you want to know who wrote that book,
Or the name of that famous TV cook.
If you're unsure of how to spell a word,
Or need the name of that unknown bird.
If you want the recipe for a Christmas cake,
Or need to know which pill to take.
For all these things, and so much more,
It just takes a knock, on my neighbour's door.

If you need to know how to fix a tap,
Or on a ceiling how to fill that gap.
At household chores, he knows what he's at,
He makes beans on toast and Hoovers the mat.
Is there anything he doesn't know?
Compared to him, all the others are slow.
He can even wire a plug, and build a shed,
He's even wise when asleep in bed.

Trust me
I'm a GENIUS

If you can't remember how to dance,
Or know the capitals of Spain or France.
What is the name of that lively tune?
Or the maker of that that silver spoon.
Who won that race in eighty seven?
Or the quickest way to get to Devon.
For all these things and so much more,
It just takes a knock on my neighbour's door.

His wife and daughter just dote on him,
As do his niece, and brother in law Jim.
His good friend Ron, when things he needs to know,
Always knows just where to go,
This wise man's wife admits to all who call,
That her husband is a know it all.
So if you want to know, who, or why, or what, or when,
Just knock on his door and ask for Ken.

The Fashion King of Kimberworth Park

I have always been a fashion King,
And always bought the latest thing.
I was proud to wear my yellow cords.
My orange shirt was cool beyond words.
I always thought that my clothes were great,
That a keen sense of fashion was my fate.
I was dressed to kill as a single gent,
With Rupert trousers wider than a tent.

I have always had a great fashion sense,
With none of your shirts for fifty pence,
Shirts with lace frills, in nineteen sixty eight,
At twenty one, I thought I looked great,
My wardrobe was packed with stunning arrays,
Of kipper ties and flares, from happier days.
I'd go out for a drink, on a Saturday night.
All decked out in the latest black and white.

Idyllic days of fashion, in my youthful days.
When Tootal ties, were the latest craze.
With my checked sports Jacket, and winkle picker shoes,
I was every girl's dream, so how could I lose,
I was a fashion king, and thought I looked grand,
But something was wrong, but I didn't understand.
What I learned in later years, I really should have known,
A wife picks a man's clothes, as well as her own.

No more narrow checked trousers and loud pink shirts,
To throw out my treasured clothes, now that really hurts.
I'd only been married, barely one week and a day,
When out went my Rupert's, what a colourful array
My orange shirt, and my yellow cords went next,
I have to admit I was so extremely vexed.
Even my bright lime green trunks, in which I went swimming,
In fact all of my clothes, that were so attractive to women.

What can I say, with all my confidence gone?
I'm not like that far away vision, of fashion king Ron,
My last three suits have been chosen by women,

And I've nothing to wear, with which to go swimming.
Once I was known as top of the pops,
Now all my clothes come from charity shops.
I'm older now; I don't worry these days, and try to keep calm,
I now wear clothes for comfort, and clothes that are warm.

Ron's Bad Hair Day

There's none in this group has anything to say,
About what it means to have a real bad hair day.
I lost my hair on a summer's afternoon,
At nineteen years old, in the middle of June.
When you hear about it now, you can have a good laugh.
How I lost my hair, whilst having a bath.

I soaked in the bath for over an hour,
The reason for this is that you can't read in the shower.
I'd read all my Sci-Fi about Martians and space ships,
And dream about supper and a nice plate of fish and chips.
Looking back now, reminds me that life's really not fair,
For when I emptied the bath, it was full of my hair.

The very next morning, whilst fitting a hinge,
My mates were appearing, to look at my fringe.
It was two inch further back, than it had been the day before,
It still lay in the bath, and not on the barber's shop floor.
How could a teenager go to the pub, or a dance at the Carlton,
With a haircut that resembled, the great Bobby Charlton.

Over the years I've faced ridicule and sneers,
From family and friends, and some of my peers.
But now things have changed, at the coming of a new age.
For haircuts like mine, are now all the rage.
With my brothers, and friends, I can have the last laugh,
They all have less hair than me, as I read in my bath.

A Fight with a Bear

Barry the boxer with his mates at the fair,
Barry the boxer had a fight with a bear.
The bear was in chains, in the ring with his promoter,
A man called Flash Harry, with a new red ford motor.
Harry was a man with plenty to say,
Who's brave enough to fight Bruno, for a ten pound note today.

When Barry stepped forward, his mates thought he'd gone funny,
But Barry was skint, and needed the money.
He'd boxed many men, and knocked them all out,
And as Barry stepped forward, the crowds started to shout.
We'll come to your funeral, and we'll invite the Mayor.
You've no chance at all, in fighting that bear.

Now Barry had a secret, known by just a select few,
His parent had been keepers, in a far off country zoo.
With his sisters and brothers, he'd fed the animals there,
But his particular favourite, had been one Bruno the bear.
When he steeped in that ring, Bruno recognised his friend,
And that wise old bear, knew how to pretend.

It was just a game, they had played long ago.
And they both decided, to put on a show.
Barry quickly went down, with a clunk and a smack,
But soon dear Bruno, lay flat on his back.
Get up said Flash Harry, you're much bigger by far,
If you lose me this fight, I'll have to flog my house and my car.

But shamed and defeated, Flash Harry ran away,
Leaving angry crowds, with unpaid bets that day.
The future for Barry and Bruno, was rosy and fine.
Repeating their act nightly was a little gold mine.
Barry made millions, at the Rotherham Town Fair,
All through the friendship, between Barry, and Bruno the bear.

A Window in Time

The window was invented in 5000 BC,
By an unknown English man, by the name of Billy Bree.
Billy was the first inventor, to live upon this earth.
His parents had chosen Yorkshire, as the place of Billy's birth.
To live in sunny Rotherham, had been his father's dream,
So his son could play for Yorkshire's, famous rock throwing team.

But his father's dreams were shattered, by Billy's attitude,
Billy had been brought up proper and never known to be rude.
I'd rather live in Barnsley, than play that rock throwing game,
I'd even live in Chesterfield, and invent a window frame.
That was too much for his father, that proud Yorkshire man,
If you stay and invent in Rotherham me lad, I'll help you all I can.

So in a cave they named the Domino, they both set up shop,
And invented many useful things, until darkness bade them stop.
Those short dark days in the winter, their livelihood did hinder,
So Billy said to his father we'd better invent that window.
It will give us extra hours of light, if we place a window higher,
And if we want to work after dark, we must also invent some fire.

Using sharpened flint as tools, was not an easy game.
But with much perseverance, they made that first window frame.
Fame came quite quickly, to that creative father and his son,
They became very wealthy, for every cave soon wanted one.
They lived in a close community, and were never alone,
Money had not been invented, so they were paid in lumps of stone.

Rocks and stones were scattered, causing many trips and falls,
Until Billy and his father, invented dry stone walls.
They built them around the village, and laid stones on the road,
But Father had a brainwave "we'll build a stone abode"
But Billy was the brainy one and he always had plenty of nous,
Stone abode sounds silly dad, so let's call this place a house.

Building walls perfected, it soon became their game,
And into each new house they included, a door and window frame.
They built hundreds of new houses, and the years soon came to pass,
Those window frames improved in time, when Billy invented glass.
They built the Domino as their very first pub, and found it quite a lark,
In those happy far off peaceful days, in the stone age Kimberworth Park.

Bread and Jam

In the middle of a wood there lives a man,
Whose only love is bread and jam.
When he was a baby his mother tried,
To change his diet but he only cried.
She tempted him with all things fried,
But he choked on a sausage and nearly died.
A bottle he had whilst in his pram,
Until he discovered bread and jam.

When at Redscope school his teacher said,
You'll not grow strong on jam and bread,
You need some meat and potatoes too,
Apple pies and good beef stew.
The dinner lady, Elsie Fipps,
Tempted him with fish and chips.
Fried pork chops, and eggs and ham,
But the lad held out for bread and jam.

His poor old dad tried a different route
And tempted him with lots of fruit.
Apples and pears and a nice big plum.
But dad gave up trying and sent for his mum.
Who sent him for a psychological test,
While both she and her husband had a rest
They tried to wean him from bread, jam, and butter,
But there was nothing they could do to help this nutter.

On leaving school this teenage nut,
Went to work at Pizza Hut.
At a local store in Rotherham,
He was banned from eating bread and jam.
Pizzas were the company rule,
And bread and jam was not seen as cool.
And Sam as this young man was known,
Went down to only seven stone.

He left this job as soon as he could,
And went to live in Redscope wood.
He made a living by painting scenes,

Of the local church on St. John's green.
Of the Haynook and the Domino pub,
And with the money he bought his grub.
Was it chips or was it ham?
Not on your nelly it was bread and jam.

He's still hidden away and rarely seen,
But can still be found if you're patient and keen.
On summer evenings, just before it gets dark,
If you happen to be passing through Barkers Park.
If the weather is fine, and ne'er a cloud,
Go into the woods and shout out loud,
Are you there, or hey up Sam
And you might just be offered, some bread and Jam.

Celia's Buns

I've never been on a river cruise,
Studied Latin or been on the news.
I've never been on those Great North Runs,
But I've eaten many of Celia's buns,

I've never cycled to Timbuktu,
Sailed on a yacht as one of the crew.
Never skated all day on frozen lakes,
But I've eaten my share of Celia's cakes.

I've never yodelled at dawn from a mountain top
Drunk two gallon of Ben Shaw's fizzy pop
Never admired a gorilla's eyes
But I've eaten dozens of Celia's mince pies

Eating Celia's Pastry is like a dream come true,
It can be eaten with custard, and strawberry ice cream too.
To see husband Ken in action, is quite a surprise.
Eating a plateful of Celia's fruit pies.

Coming Home from School

Coming home from school on washday, on Mondays in my youth,
Was a horrible experience, if I were to tell the truth.
Steam filled all the kitchen, and wet clothes everywhere,
My mother up to her eyes in soap suds was more than I could bear.

Hard work for my mother, as she struggled all year through,
To provide us with our clean clothes, with never a thank you,
Washing, ironing, cleaning, cooking, was sadly hers to do.
Before washers were invented, electric irons and cookers too.

Coming home for lunch on washday, was certainly not cool,
But poor mum was trapped at home, when I went back to school.
I remember mum with fondness, for all she did for us,
A lady from that generation, who did not make a fuss.

I look back upon it all in hindsight, how I often led her a merry dance.
There were many things that she'd have liked to do, but never got the chance.
If only I could turn the clock back, and help her with some chore,
Oh to be coming home for one last time, to see my mum once more.

Coming Home from Italy

We've scrimped and saved all year long, to go on holiday,
We've read all the brochures, and we've found a place to stay.
Our excitement builds, as the special day draws near,
We're looking forward to our posh hotel, to the sun,
Fine foods and a cool glass of beer.

Our tour guide Sally is the best, and together with our driver Lawrence,
Take us to see Lake Garda, on to Pisa and then to Florence.
We never want to leave this place, with the weather dry and sunny,
We'd carry on all year long, if we only had the money.

They say all good things come to an end, even wine, women and song,
Of course my wife disagrees with me, says it's not where I belong.
We've seen Italy's many wonders from Pompeii, to Sienna and Rome,
But after fourteen days of coach and plane, at last we're coming home.

The Ballad of Ricky Clay

As I walked along the sea shore, upon a summers day.
I happened upon a wise old man, whose name was Ricky Clay.
Ricky was a strange old man, and his clothes were far from new,
His suit was bright yellow, and he only wore one shoe.

He spoke with a Yorkshire accent, and often said e by gum,
I warmed to him quite quickly, for he sounded like my mum.
He was full of wise sayings, like if you meet wild dogs don't bother-em,
With such wisdom that he possessed, I knew he came from Rotherham.

Ricky Clay from down our way, is only sixty three,
His hair is like a bale of hay, and muscles like a tree.
Depending how you treat him, he will either love or hate yer
His wisdom comes from studying, the whole of human nature.

He comes back to Rotherham, once a month each year,
He visits local chip shops and samples local beer.
He visits Kimberworth library to meet the reader's group

He tells them of his travels and how to make oak leaf soup

He goes about the countryside, imparting of his knowledge,
He never went to proper school, he never went to college.
But people seek him out, for his advice, even to this day,
That wise and yellow suited, one shoe man, the legendary Ricky Clay.

Celia's drawer Lament

There are thirty eight drawers in our house and that I find fantastic.
Two of metal, fourteen of wood and the rest are made of plastic.
Drawers are special things, to cherish throughout your life.
And should be shared equally, between a husband and his wife.

Ken made a splendid chest, with twelve drawers made of wood,
And filled eleven drawers with his possessions, as only Kenneth could.
The unfairness of this action, beggar's belief, but it is a fact of life,
He only allocated one small drawer, to Celia his neglected wife.

But this tale has an unhappy ending, which simply was a disgrace,
For in Celia's one and only drawer, she discovered Ken's glasses case.
This caused an upset for that poor lady of proportions off the scale,
So in retaliation, she went on Amazon, and put his scroll saw up for sale.

Ken was distraught and bewildered, at what his wife had done,
So he did what he'd always done, and consulted his friend Ron.
Now Ron was wise and resourceful, and well known for his tact,
But for once he surprised his friend Ken, for it was Celia that he backed.

They discussed the subject all that night, and through the following day,
When you treat your wife unfairly, said our Ron, you often have to pay,
You promised her your worldly goods, so she has what once was yours,
So if you want a quiet life, Kenneth me lad, keep out of Celia's drawers

Flowers I have eaten

Most people have gardens full of flowers, because they look so sweet,
But the flowers in my garden are only there to eat.
I've studied them in detail, and know every component part,
Even Albert Einstein, wouldn't know where to start.
I don't need supermarkets any more, or shop in them for hours,
All my carbohydrates and proteins are provided by my flowers.
You may think that I am crazy, and even start to laugh,
For I even grow geraniums, in my mother's old tin bath.

I supplement my flowers with fruit and veg, and get my five a day,
And I benefit from all this food and never have to pay.
Flowers are my favourite plant, and I've eaten quite a few.
I put poppies in Lasagne, and cowslips in my stew.
I mix daisies with my carrots, and add lupins to my mash,
If you are tempted by my recipes, then why not have a bash.
For lunch on Sunday afternoon, my Yorkshire pud I cook,
With juice extracted from an eggplant, as in my special book.

I have a balanced diet, of fruit, veg, and flowers,
I experiment with plants each day, and while away the hours.
For supper I eat begonias, and cabbage leaves I fry,
For pudding I have rose hip wine, with potato and bluebell pie.
My meals are full of colour, like my famous rainbow flan,
I make it out of clematis flowers, in multi coloured pan.

My neighbours think I'm a hippy, because of my multi coloured life,
Well if they think I'm weird, they should come and meet my wife.

One thing I have failed to do, and I admit to my mistake,
I never have succeeded to bake a wallflower, and a sweet pea cake.
Some foods are not always available, and that's for an obvious reason,
Flowers such a daffodils and bluebells, are restricted to one season.
As I have already stated, the neighbours think I'm a multi coloured hippy,
But I often go incognito, when I sneak to the local chippy,
Each day I keep fit and healthy, and as I run about the room,
My legs are now covered in rose petals, and my ears have begun to bloom.

Jim the woodsman

Down a country lane there walked, a man all dressed in black and green,
He was the finest woodsman that this country's ever seen.
He could fell a tree in half an hour, with a saw and axe so bright,
But he much preferred to fell a tree, by using dynamite.
He was famous for his hand made stools, made from good old English oak.
He sold them for seven and sixpence, to local peasant folk.

His name was Jim the forester, and his lovely wife called Mel,
Who sang in a choir in their domain, and did so very well.
He did gardening for the old folk, in bonny Rotherham Town,
He'd work all day for two and six or in the evening for half a crown.
He'd save shiny florins in a barrel, and when the cask was full.
He'd buy a brand new wagon, his donkey for to pull.
Our Jim was a fitness freak and also quite a menace,
He'd tell jokes to an audience whilst playing table tennis.
In the morning he'd visit a gymnasium, which was named after him,
He'd then run back home again, and was known as speedy Jim.
Once a week he'd visit a local hostelry, come sun or snow or hail,
To eat Yorkshire puddings and sausages and a drink a pint of Theakston's ale

Jim was a gangly outdoors man as handsome as he was tall.
He often walked with a group of friends and invented 'Spot the Ball'.
They walked each week on a Wednesday morn and were a merry band,
And when in the fields they crossed a stile, Jim gave the girls a hand.
They were the finest walkers, this land has ever seen.
Led by local walk leaders and a man dressed in black and green.

The Joys of Decorating

Decorating is such a delight,
Painting doors from morning till night.
Undercoat on and then the gloss,
Working all day long to please the boss.

Stripping walls, will that suit her?
I'd rather play on my computer
Mix the paste and stick the paper,
Love it all, what a caper.

Painting and papering are all done,
Now is the time to have some fun.
But now I have that funny feeling,
That I forgot to paint the kitchen ceiling.

Choosing the colour, not on your life,
My choice comes third after my daughter and wife.
It doesn't match the curtains or suite.
How can a simple man ever compete?

Decorating is such a delight,
Hurrah it's finally Saturday night.
No painting on Sunday she's left in the lurch,
No painting to do when I'm at the church.

My friend Ken likes decorating too,
We both tell our wives there's no more to do.
We've approached our tasks with the upmost of feeling,
You're not done yet, there's that crack in the ceiling

We get out the filler and putty knives too,
We're really uncertain what we have to do.
We apply the caulking from our mastic gun,
Filling gaps in ceilings is so much fun.

My magic train spotter's hat

I put a hat upon my head and I vanished out of sight,
It was a magic hat you see, and I wore it every night.
You may think I was invisible, but that was not the case,
The hat had just transported me, to a very different place.

I found that hat in Rotherham Town, in a Heart Foundation shop,
It was amongst many other hats, on a shelf right at the top.
It had been there for many years, so one pound I did pay,
It never worked for other folk, for they wore it during the day.

The hat did not endear itself, to people in that shop,
It was pink with yellow and white spots on, with a train stuck on the top.
But when I looked upon that hat, something caught my eye,
It had a magic spell on it, so that hat I had to buy.

Why hadn't it been bought before, is a question you may ask,
It came as a part of a set you see, with an anorak and a flask.
It had belonged to a magic train spotter, a cross eyed man called Bruce,
And could only be sold to a fellow spotter, and one the hat did choose.

The secret of this magic hat, I will try to explain to you,
I put this hat on late at night, and appeared in nineteen sixty two.
I appeared in very bright sunlight, on a platform on a railway station,
It was a different platform every night, much to my elation.

I had a note book with my numbers in, and every name had written,
After many months of spotting, I had visited every place in Britain.
I was the envy of train buffs everywhere, and my fame will never fade,
For after twelve months of spotting, I had seen every loco ever made.

My friends today wouldn't believe me, though I've only got a few.
For the only place that I can prove it, is in nineteen sixty two.
I still go there quite often, though nobody ever knows,
I don't go to spot trains any more, but go to buy very cheap sixties clothes.

How do I get back home, is something you may ask,
I have to take my anorak off, and drink the contents of my flask.
I may dispose of my hat one day, and my adventures then will stop.
Then you too can buy my hat, at the Heart Foundation shop.

My Working Life

Work for some people is a joy to behold,
For others it's a lifetime of doing what you're told.
Doing a job which you love is full of joy and thrills.
But for most people it's a means, of paying all the bills.

In my early working life, I enjoyed working with wood,
And drew intense pleasure, when creating something good.
Cutting dovetails and tenons, making cupboards and doors
Enjoying making things, that other considered chores.

The affinity with tools and hardwood, is a lifetime affair,
Carving exotic pew ends, or making a dog leg stair.
Sharp steel on wood, is a craftsman's delight,
When working from early morning, and far into the night.

But the time comes when priorities change, and the joy seems to fade.
Supporting a family then comes first, and bills need to be paid.
You still do your work, and gain pleasure by a job well done.
But the joy of long hours creating, no longer seems to be much fun.

But in the third stage in life, if you only admit the truth,
You work again for pleasure, and regain something of your youth.
Old skills are recaptured, by working with your hands once again.
Retirement is a pleasure, if you can put up with the pain.

My dream Holiday

My dream Holiday would have to be,
A tour of the world for my wife and me.
To see the seven wonders, or those that still remain,
And travel through the continents, on a famous steam train.

If I was long haired, and a young man once again.
I'd pose on the beaches, in far off sunny Spain.
But now I'm short of hair, and almost far too old,
I go each year on holiday, and drive to where I am told.

There are a number of places, that I would like to see,
If I was a young man again, both rich and fancy free.
I'd visit the pyramids of Egypt, and see the mighty sphinx.
Much better than washing dishes, stood at kitchen sinks.

To see once again works of art, in Florence's fair city,
And appear to all the ladies, as someone who's quite witty.
Or live on a coral island, surrounded by warm seas.
And live on the produce, from luxurious tropical trees.

Or visit ancient ruins, in far off distant lands,
Or dig for pirate's treasure, on warm golden sands.
An archaeologist on television, I would long to be,
And travel the world over, with the good old BBC.

I'd fly to New Zealand, on a plane with very large wings,
To see where they filmed the Hobbit, and Lord of the Rings.
But to be entirely honest I've only saved a few quid,
So I'll have to be content this year, with a holiday in Brid.

Who is the very first?

An historian or archaeologist, is what I'd choose to be,
I think about it every day, from noon till half past three.
I'd specialise in discovering, who was the very first,
This would be a difficult task, but I'd try until I burst.
Who was the first to discover fire, or build a wall of stone,
I'd find the very first caveman's axe, and keep it for my own,.

I'd study from the age of ten, and read many books and think,
Who was the very first person, to write with pen and ink?
I'd meet many famous people, wearing polished shoes or wellies,
Some of them would be on Time Team that we see on our telly's
I'd dig for Roman artefacts in Britain, Italy and Bahrain,
I'd find the first minted coin, and the first woodworker's plane.

I'd write the history of first things, and be as happy as can be,
When I discover the first person, who first chopped down a cedar tree.
The first person to use a spanner, and fly and airplane.
And who first discovered seams of coal, and who used it on a train
I'd learn who first made trousers, to cover up their knees,

Ronald Town

Was the person who invented the needle and thread, a lady called Denise?

I'd dig in ancient Egypt, and discover Pharaoh's tombs,
And discover gold and silver, in subterranean rooms.
Who first made wheels with spokes in, I'd discover in that place,
And discover Cleopatra's wedding dress, made linen and of lace.
I'd read all the famous cookery books, and discover if I could,
The person who became famous, by making Yorkshire pud.

I'd discover who invented fish and chips, and made tomato sauce,
Or who was the first jockey, to ride upon a horse.
Who invented porcelain, and made the first dinner plate.
Or the very first carpenter, to make a garden gate.
I'd have the time of my life, discovering who made things first,
Like who made the first barrel of beer, to quench their ancient thirst.

I'd find the first painting, in some unknown British cave,
And if I'm lucky I'll also discover, the very first man to have a shave.
I'd have loved to live this enchanted life, of strawberries and cream,
But I know that it's too late now, and it is just a dream.
But my life so far I don't regret, and this will make amends,
I wouldn't miss one moment now, among my dearest friends.

The Yorkshire Time Traveller

Fred the Yorkshire time traveler visited the universe in a shed.
His first visit was to a world where skies were all bright red
He then visited a world where the trees were only just budding,
Then came back to Rotherham, for his mother's Yorkshire pudding.
He was born in the thirteenth century the son of country squire,
He trained in the use of weapons and arrows he did fire.

He'd lived many years and had seen many sights,
He lived during the war of the roses, and had been in many fights.
During one tiring battle, as he longed for his bed,
A hillside just exploded, revealing a weird looking shed.
Fred approached the shed carefully with a certain amount of dread
Not realising that this wooden hut was a time traveller's shed.

To open that shed door, our Fred he tried his hardest,
When landing beside him suddenly was Dr Who's TARDIS.
You've discovered a lost time machine said the Doctor to our Fred

But first let's get away from this battle, before we both end up dead.
They entered the police box together and accompanied by a strange sound,
And materialized inside the new time machine that our Fred had just found.

By the authority of a Time Lord, Doctor Who said,
You are now an honorary Time Lord, and I'm giving you this shed.
To travel through time and space, doing good to all types of creatures,
But before I leave you I'll explain, your time machine's best features.
The chameleon circuit is broken; that means it's kaput and its dead,
For the rest of your life it will always be, disguised as a garden shed.

The Doctor explained how to work this new shed,
It's a series fifty time machine which meant nowt to our Fred.
You can go where you like, be you happy or be you glum,
But once every year back to Yorkshire you certainly must come,
The secret of a Time Lord's long life, I can now to you reveal,
Is eating Yorkshire Pudding, at the annual Christmas meal.

Worst ever Christmas presents

At Christmastime long ago, when I was almost six,
I badly wanted a big red car, but I got some wooden bricks.
I wrote to Father Christmas, and put in a complaint,
We've no cars left replied Santa, and so he sent a tin of paint.
It's the same colour as my bedroom door, I told my mum that day,
That Santa doesn't miss a trick, was all she had to say.

When I was eight, I was asked what I would like,
I answered immediately, and said, it's got to be a bike,
A bike's too dear said mother, you'll have to think again.
The bike went up the spout that day, and I got a clock work train.
I was happy to get a train, that was painted green and black,
But when it came it was no use, for they couldn't afford the track.

I wanted a painting set about the age of ten,
With watercolours and brushes, and a permanent black pen.
But instead I got box of games, and a pair of shoes that were too bright,
I hated games with a passion, and the shoes they were too tight,
When I complained to mum and dad, they sent me straight to bed.
Why ask me what I really want, when no one listens to what I said.

At fourteen I asked for a tool set, from the club book we had at home,
Please don't let me down, this time dad, and buy me a garden gnome.
Or buy me clothes that I don't like, a record or a pair of football boots,
Or a Roy Rogers cowboy outfit, with a gun that never shoots.
But to my surprise I got my tools, and didn't feel so daft.
But I started my job as a joiner that year, and mum and dad both laughed.

Once at work the presents stopped, and this was a relief to me,
No more useless presents, I've had since the age of three.
I've never been jealous of my two brothers; I'd never go that far,
But the very year I started work, my brother got a big bright red car.
My other brother also was asked, what he would really like,
And to my surprise he got that year, a brand new two wheel bike.

My wife's won the lottery

It was one morning in June that changed my life,
It began with scream from darling wife.
I've won five million pounds, was all she could say,
I put two quid on the lottery, just the other day.
Now this was a shock, the biggest one so far,
I can have a big house now, and a shining new car.

I could drive my red Ferrari in Italy and Spain,
And when I come back home, I would buy a big steam train.
I'd buy a cottage in Scarborough, and all my friends I'd invite,
It would have fifteen large bedrooms, all painted apple white.
The things we could do with five million in cash,
I've never been sailing, but I can now have a bash.

Now don't get too excited, just try and stay calm,
I'm spending my lottery winnings, on a nice big country farm.
We've got to plan our future, and not waste all this cash,
I can't talk to you now my dear, to the bank I must dash.
She knows what she's doing, no need for alarm.
But do I want to really live, in a smelly old country farm.

The things I could do with half of that money,
I'd help my family and friends, and my days would be sunny.

Wait till she comes back home, I will try and makes her see sense.
I don't want to spend my days spreading manure, or mending a broken fence
She came back all excited, and this started all the rows,
She'd spent all the money on a farm, and a herd of two hundred cows

What about my new cars, and holidays in the sun,
Milking cows at dawn, is not my idea of fun.
Planting crops in the spring, I just aint gonna do,
And the best place for animals is in London zoo.
The money had all gone now, and so I started to scream,
Then I woke up in bed, to find it was only a dream.

The Eternal Optimist

I hope I'm not late for work again it is a fear of mine
My train was due at eight O'clock and now it's ten past nine.
I am an eternal optimist my glass is always half full.
But I hope my train takes me to Brid, and not to blinking Hull

I hope my boss will understand, if I am late once again
I run courses in positive thinking so I hope I catch my train.
I am an eternal optimist my glass is always half full.
But although my job pays really well it is a load of bull.

I hope these trousers still fit me, and I don't need a bigger size
Maybe I should change my diet and not live on chips and pies.
I am an eternal optimist my glass is always half full.
But I'll buy trousers with an elastic waist, when I get to Brid or Hull.

I hope I don't fall asleep while travelling on this train.
And when I get to Bridlington, it doesn't start to rain
I am an eternal optimist my glass is always half full.
I've forgotten my umbrellas I always buy in Hull.

I never used to be like this, so worried and uncertain,
I'd never watch a horror film from behind the front room curtain.
I am an eternal optimist my glass is always half full.
But while I've been pondering, I've arrived in blinking Hull.

I've just had a text message from my boss, and my eyes are getting full.

He's given up all hope on me, and transferred my job to Hull.
I am an eternal optimist my glass is always half full.
But I've grown rather fond of Brid and I'm not so sure of Hull.

My Keys are Missing

I'm late for that meeting and I am ill at ease,
I wish I could remember, where I've put my blooming keys.
I ask my darling wife, but of course it is no use,
You'd lose your head, my lad if only it were loose.
Where did you have them last, then she said to me?
If I knew that woman, you know that's where I'd be.

I've looked in my coats and trousers and even in my shoes,
Of all the times and days, for my keys for to lose.
Peter's on the telephone the meetings just begun,
Being a church secretary is certainly not much fun.
Start without me I say, I'll be a quick as I can be,
In desperation I'd better try, down the back of the settee.

Use you spare set my wife cries out,
I've lost them too, and I start to shout.
Lower your voice don't shout at me,
It's not me who's lost their keys.
Not having my keys just now is such a wrench,
Off to the garage once again, to look on the joiner's bench

I empty out the waste bin and cause a stink,
Did you have to do it in the kitchen sink?
I move all the furniture including that heavy chair,
I find 50p and a ginger nut but my keys are not there.
It was then I remembered, just where my keys are,
I left them in the ignition, for I never locked the car.

I get to church quite quickly but the meeting it is over,
To find the vicar is just getting into, her brand new shiny Rover.
Hello there, I'm sorry I'm late the vicar hears me shout,
Don't worry, It'll not happen again Ron, you've just been voted out.
I go home happy and ecstatic, singing and so full of glee,
There'll be no taking notes again, or typing minutes for me.

Cowboy Builders

Jack the bricklayer tall and blonde
Built a house near our local pond.
He built it nearer than he oughta
And put his garage in the water.
Instead of cars that wouldn't float
Inside he kept a rowing boat.

Pete the plumber small and thick
Put in a sink all made of brick.
He built it higher than he should
In the middle of the local wood.
In the sink were many gaps
And nowhere to connect his taps.

Ron the joiner young and merry
Went to work in scarf and beret.
He led his master quite a dance
Looking like a lad from France.
His only tool was a brace and bit
His master told him what to do with it.

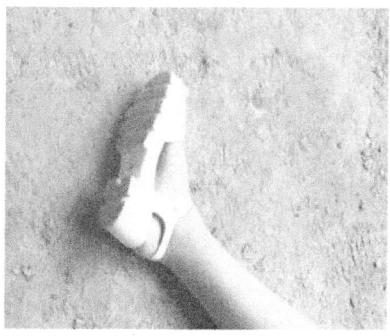

Dave the plasterer broad and tall
Spread his plaster on the wall.
To him this was the thing to do
But he spread it with his girlfriend's shoe.
He gave the foreman quite a shock
By making it smooth with his sock.

Maurice the electrician tall and wise
Gave his wife quite a surprise.

By wiring up her freshly baked bread
She thought he'd gone funny in the head.
When cutting a slice it gave her a fright
By switching on the kitchen light.
No more wiring for you, said his poor wife
Grow up lad and get a life.

The Man who never shaves

In a land beneath the waves lives a man who never shaves.
He was born to parents who, lived on fish and never stew.
Fish was dear so they did save, and buy a des res under water cave
People thought that they were weird, because mother and son grew a beard

In a land beneath the waves lives a man who never shaves.
His beard is as long as it can get that once he used it as fishing net.
Cod and herring he has caught, and a dozen squid with ne'er a thought
Dog fish too that never bark, until one day he caught a shark.

It pulled his beard and dragged him far, in that under water tug of war.
From Whitby harbour to Japan, and back to where it first began.

The old man thought he'd had his lot, when the shark got tied up in a knot.
Learn a lesson from this man so brave, and every morning have a shave.

Patron Saint

I heard this story from my dad
On a night that was wet and dark.
He told me that our Patron Saint
Was really born on Kimberworth Park.
He said it was a family secret
Passed down from father to son.
And as I was the one hundredth descendant
I must now tell everyone.
All this happened Long ago
Even before dogs had learned to bark.
When a lad called George was born to a poacher
Who lived on ancient Kimberworth Park.

George learned all the tricks from his father
And with a longbow he became an ace,
He shot deer and rabbits and squirrels,
And caught pheasants by the brace.
He learned to wrestle and fight with his fists
And to fight with sword and spear.
Until he became famous throughout the land
And the king of him did hear.
He sent his emissary to Rotherham
And bid George to come to the royal palace.
George replied, I'll come if I can bring my sheepdog Ben,
And my pretty young wife called Alice.

Now young George had a whale of a time,
With King Edgar and all his mates.
And every evening he would sign autographs,
Outside the palace gates.
King Edgar was very proud of George,
And thought his manner so quaint,
And within six months our canny Yorkshire lad,
Was made England's second Patron Saint.
He went on a state tour of England,

Along with Alice and sheepdog Ben,
And on his return to London,
He lived in Downing Street at number ten.

But back home things were not the same;
Things had gone from bad to worse,
And folk back there on Kimberworth Park
Seemed to be living under a curse.
The cause of all this upset was Ceredig,
a mighty Green Welsh Dragon,
Who had settled on a hilltop near Kimberworth manor
Behind a brewers wagon.
The people rallied round to fight him,
But couldn't do a thing,
And after all else had failed to work,
They pleaded with Edgar their king.

Edgar sent for George that evening,
And told of this tragic news
So George gathered men together,
With bows made from the finest English yews.
With Alice and Ben beside him
He set out for Kimberworth Park.
And to boost the morale of George and his army
Ben his sheepdog had started to bark
He landed back home on a Wednesday
And met up with mum, dad and his mates.
And by early Thursday morning
He was camped by the manor house gates.

Ceredig started to attack them,
And singed the hair of many a man,
Until George invented the helmet,
By using his mother's copper saucepan.
Green Dragon stood defiantly
On top of hill where pub now stands today
The proud English bowmen started firing,
And continued firing arrows all that day.
While George sneaked up behind dragon
And pierced his heart with his broad sword,
He toppled off hill with Ben barking,
But Green Dragon never again said a word.

From that day George was a hero
And celebrated throughout this proud land.
And venison and chips were on the menu,
Jelly and custard and a thirty piece band.
It was the 23rd of April when it happened
Which is now known as St. George's Day
And each year on the eve of that great victory
We eat pie and peas together at Green Dragon
And only four pound to Pay.
No one now remembers where George fought this battle
Or the story of Alice and Ben.
But I sometimes hear a sheepdog barking,
When I visit the Green Dragon pub now and then.

Ronald Town

Paper

Paper was invented by the Egyptians in the third century BC,
Made from papyrus or the bark of the fig, mulberry and also the Daphne tree
It revolutionised the world back then, and does the same today
Some paper products are expensive but willingly we pay.
It has so many uses, and it's not as simple as it looks,
It's used for writing letters, and making wallpaper and also reading books.
Without paper creative writing groups, would certainly cease to exist,
With nothing to write our poems on it surely would be missed.

We'd struggle in our painting group if paper was not there
Without paper in our libraries the shelving would be bare.
If we wrote and painted on plywood just think what we'd have to pay
The origami masters from the orient would all be out of work today.
Paper makes life much better and nothing could be finer
And paper that we know today was invented in 1st century China
The Chinese and Japanese use it for their houses, up to the present day
But with the British climate, a paper house, would certainly wash away.

There is a strange rumour, hereabout, that paper was invented near this place
By an ancient Yorkshire lad with woad upon his face
He was the village idiot and his name was Michael Ugman Bevan,
He spent his time carving his name on trees, until he was eleven.
There had to be a better way, than this tree engraving caper,
It was wearing away his finger nails, so he invented tree bark paper.
He boiled mulched up bark in cooking pots, much to his mother's ire,
But the mixture soon dried out, beside the kitchen fire.

The resultant paper soon dissolved, Michael's mothers rage,
It was heralded the greatest thing, and the marvel of the age,.
He made his fame and fortune, and became richer than good king Will,
And he went on to invent pen and ink, which made him richer still.
Now you may think that this is pure fiction, and a bit of a lark,
But from that day you never saw, his name carved on any oak tree bark.
To say that the Chinese invented paper in AD 127
Is an insult to the memory of Michael Ugman Bevan.

Go Carts on Kimberworth Park

Over fifty years I can see it still,
Our home-made go cart speeding down the hill.
This wooden wonder O what a joy,
The proud possession of any boy.
A set of pram wheels was the start,
Of this nineteen fifties sleek go cart.
A pair of wheels nailed to the plank,
Is far better than money in the bank.

An orange box fixed at the rear,
In front, are wheels from which to steer.
A rope attached and then we're ready,
Our new go cart is strong and steady.
Down the hill the risks we take,
Too late now to fit a brake.
We level out come to a stop,
And buy sweets from our local shop.

Chewing sweets what a thrill
Then drag the trolley back up the hill
Out of breath we never learn,
We just can't wait for our next turn,
It's getting late and time for bed,
Our new go cart's in the shed.
A fitting garage for our new toy,
A lovely time to be a young boy.

School Days

When I started school as a little lad it was in days of old
You spoke only when spoken to and did what you were told.
If you broke the rules at school you never did so again
For you often got the slipper, or the dreaded teacher's cane.
I got the cane twice myself, and it certainly left its mark,
I learned a valuable lesson then, of knowing when not to talk.

Apart from the punishment, my Junior School I did enjoy,
I played with my mates at playtime like any normal boy.
I loved history, craft and literature and singing my favourite hymn
Junior school was marvellous, and it was there I learned to swim.
At all sport I was terrible, but I loved to paint and draw,
And making things from balsa wood, with a fine bladed saw.

At eleven I went to secondary school, and walked there with my mates,
But all the laughter and fun ended, as we entered our school gates.
Who made the rules at this new school; I bet that no one knows,
You couldn't run in corridors, or wear your choice of clothes.
The teachers had their favourites, like David, Ian or James,
The rest of us did not exist; we were the ones who hated games.

The lessons that I loved were History, literature, science and art,
I hated geography and sport most of all, and dreaded taking part,
But the highlight of the week for me, was making things with wood,
I'd saw and plane all afternoon, if the teacher said I could.
I wanted to study geology, and make myself a name,
But qualifications I had none, and a joiner I became.

Looking back now in hindsight now, school set me up for life
I learned to love the written word in common with my wife.
The skills I learned in woodwork I remember to this day,
How to sharpen planes and chisels, and saw wood the proper way.
I meet old school mates every week, and our friendship will always last,
 And all the things I didn't like from school, are now faded into the past.

<u>My Sporting Achievements</u>

Why couldn't I play football like many of my mates, I tried to as a lad?
Each year I had a case ball, at Christmas, from my mum and dad.
I'd kick it in a straight line, to a goal at the end of the pitch,
But it would go where I didn't want it to, and end up in a ditch.

Why couldn't I play tennis like Peter, Dave or Mick,
I'd hit the ball into the net, or out of bounds I never learned the trick.
I'd always jump the wrong way, and never return the ball,
I tried all the sports as a lad, and failed at them all.

I wasn't bad at short distance running, but the javelin I liked the most.
Until I just missed the teachers head and pierced out new goal post.
The teacher decided I'd no aptitude, along with my mates Malcolm and Chris,
They sent us to the library every Tuesday, and we'd give PE a miss.

I loved all the lessons, that didn't involve a racket ball or bat,
Woodwork was a favourite, and I became quite good at that.
I loved science and history, and came the top of the class,
But Geography I really hated and hardly got a pass.

English literature was my passion, writing stories I loved best,
And surprisingly I even loved the daily English spelling test.
I couldn't wait for the PE lessons, to which my mates so longed to go,
And I'd go along to the library, and write stories of long ago.

Bungee Jumping

You need to do your daily exercise my physio said to me,
Sitting watching television all day long will aggravate your knee.
Twice a day laid on your back and on your stomach too,
If you want your hamstring to get better it's entirely up to you.
I'm bored with lifting up my leg and all that boring stuff,
So I decided to do a bungee jump and that should be enough.

Of bungee jumping as a sport I've always been a fan,
So I started in a simple way off my neighbour's caravan.
And now my physio gives me an extra workout, to fix my other knee,
Now I limp on two legs, I'm as happy as can be.
When I am cured I'm gonna have, bungee lessons from the very best,
So I asked my friend Marilyn for whom she would suggest.

I found that she was an expert, and in that sport an ace.
She lives in a place called Redcar that north eastern seaside place.
She's often jumps off Morrison's roof and bounces up and down,
She's known as Redcar's answer to Tigger, in famous northern town.
But husband Pete was furious, and with Marilyn did beg,
If those cycle inner tubes come apart, you're bound to break a leg.

So I went to her for lessons, on how to bungee jump,
But my wife Valerie put the spoke in, and gave me such a thump.
Why do you always have stupid hobbies, can't you just read a book.
Or have lessons from Mary berry, and learn how to really cook.
Now I'm sad and embarrassed, for to really tell the truth,
I've told my mates, I'm going to jump, off Marks and Spencer's roof,

The Knocker up of Old Kimberworth Circa 1900

A village near old Rotherham town was as quiet as can be,
The only noise to be heard for miles, were birds up in a tree.
No person stirred on High street, or within that village fair,
Where are all our children, all the school teachers did declare?

At Jenkins boiler works, Sir Robert said, on the stroke of ten,
I've got workers from all over, but where are my Kimberworth men?
The brickyards were half empty, on that fateful Friday morn,
When those lazy men get here, they'll wish they'd never been born.

The winding wheel at the pit was still, for those men were missing too,
And all the men stood idle for there, was nothing they could do.
The local farmer on Kimberworth Park, was in a state of panic too,
His cows needed milking at six O clock, and it was almost half past two.

Beatson Clark was just the same, for no furnace men meant no glass,
For the men who came, what could they do, but sit upon their ass.
Local iron works were depleted, for the canteen staff did not turn up,
The men had a liquid lunch at the local pub, and pale ale they did sup.

The police and military were called, and to Kimberworth they went,
They set up shop near the manor house, in a Khaki coloured tent.
They walked around those quiet streets, to assess the situation,
They said that the silence was the result, of a cunning foreign invasion

At four O clock they heard a noise, as people from their houses came,
They'd let their employers down, and would never live down the shame.
The village called a meeting, to discover who caused this situation,
Ben Roddison was the culprit, and knocking up was his occupation.

Poor Ben hid behind the backs, of son Enoch and Fanny Ben's fair wife,
 The crowd were getting angry, and Ben was fearful for his life.
Explain how this happened, said Chief Constable Gilbert Oswald Hale,
And Ben explained to police chief and his neighbours, this sad and sorry tale.

Ben was the local knocker upper, and was a conscientious man,
But the night before in the Traveller's Inn, started drinking black and tan.
After 15 pints Ben and Fanny staggered home, after having so much to sup,
And didn't get up in the morning to wake the village up.

The moral of this story is, if you want to get up for work each day,

Is to buy a new alarm clock, out of your very next week's pay.
And ban knocker up Ben and wife Fanny, from local pubs during the week,
And once again Ben was seen with pole in hand but of beer he did not reek.

So if you wanted knocking up, back then, Benjamin Roddison was your man,
For he became a reformed character and never again drank black and tan.

David the Blacksmith

David the blacksmith at his forge, in thirteen forty two,
In a hut full of smoke invented, the very first chimney flue.
It was an old bent iron pipe, connected to his furnace,
So proud of his work was David, he showed it to his wife Bernice.
But like all women of a certain argumentative type,
She wasn't at all impressed by David's bent iron pipe.
Said it was too hot; the wrong colour and the wrong size as well,
She harped on this all that week and gave husband David hell.
So David was annoyed, dejected, depressed and ended up feeling sick,
And so the very next day he invented a chimney that was all made of brick.
His wife Bernice was surprised, ecstatic, pleased and started to grovel,
Until David, annoyed and fed up, built her a fire place inside of their hovel.
The moral of this story and a warning to all men in this life,
If you invent something special don't show it to your wife.
David realized that old iron is for scrap men and those men who are thick,
So he packed in his blacksmith work and build chimneys out of brick.

Friends

Loneliness is a fact of life for many in our world today,
As children we have many friends, with whom we love to play.
Some remain friends throughout our lives,
For many of us our special friend is our husbands or our wives.

Loneliness can be overcome, and brought to an end,
All it takes is someone, who cares and wants to be our friend.
Friends are special people, the ones who always care,
The ones who at times when life is hard, you know are always there.

Friends are not perfect people, and don't always get it right.
But friends see beyond our faults and failures, and then our future's bright.
Friends often have shared interests, like creative writing, arts and crafts.
But often it's just being together, for a natter and lots of laughs.

Friendship is contagious and it often starts with one,
And one friend leads to another, and then another one.
Oh loneliness where are you now, that blight that never ends?
I've no time to be lonely now; I'm with my special friends.

I Want to Live Forever

If you could live forever, Imagine what you could see.
See all our future monarchs, and an acorn become a great tree.
If you could live forever and stay as young as a pup.
You could see a Yorkshire man wins at Wimbledon,
Or Rotherham win the FA cup.

If you could live forever, imagine what you could be.
The driver of the first No 39 hover bus
Or be a passenger on a space ship for free.
If you could live forever, imagine what you could be
The first man to reach one thousand, or own a forty foot TV.

If we could all live forever, imagine the things we would see
At our 100th birthday, we'd have another bring and share tea
Imagine if we all live forever, we'd see new steam locos once again
And visit Rotherham Station on a Saturday.
And see the Mallard in steam again

If we could live forever, none of us would have to go far
To see the first female Archbishop,
In Westminster Abbey playing an electric Guitar
The Abbey would have to be extended
I think that it would be rather good news,
To see 10,000 in the congregation
And half of them jumping up and down in the pews.

I want to live forever imagine what I could do
See all my clothes go out of fashion, and that goes for computers too.
I really don't want to live forever, imagine what I would have to do
Make sure all my unfinished jobs were completed.
For my wife has lived forever too.

Transparent Daisy and Invisible Dan

There lived a girl on St. John's Green
Who was always there but never seen.
The reason soon became apparent
Daisy Keyworth was transparent.
Daisy couldn't be seen in late afternoon or at night
But only when the sunshine, was extremely bright.

Her elder brother was a boy named Dan
He was the Kimberworth Park invisible man.
Their condition was the envy of all that they met
Especially Charlie Dowson and his pretty sister Jet.
They met at night and they fell in love
At night in the dark with no moon above.
Dan and Jet were married that year
In St. John's Church by a Reverend so dear.
You may kiss the bride said the vicar behind him
I'll do that with pleasure said Jet, if only I can find him.
I'll find you said invisible Dan on that special happy day
And if vicar can find me the wedding fees I'll pay.

Lock all the doors said the vicar all abash
He's not getting out without paying me the cash.
Now Charlie and Daisy sister of the groom,
We highly embarrassed they soon left the room.
They met in the hall and drank up their coffees
Saying when we get wed it'll be at Registry Office.

If ever at midday you're on St. John's Green
And strange things are happening and no one can be seen.
Get close to the trouble or as close as you can
And I bet you'll hear the voices of Daisy and elder brother Dan.
There's a moral to this story and its meaning is apparent
Keep away from invisible men and girls who are transparent.

In a land called Sunshine

In a land called Sunshine so long ago
Where it didn't rain and it didn't snow.
Living there was a race of tall handsome men
Whose names were all Brian, Ron or Ken.
Those ancient men they all worked like troopers
Some were railway guards or joiners and the rest were coopers.

Their women folk were wild and fierce
And every blond lady was called Denise.
Some helped their men folk making oak barrels
But only the Celias, Elaines and the carols.
In this sunny land they only worked until one
In the afternoons they enjoyed the warm summers sun.

The Denise's were exempt from all work in the city
They just had to sun bathe drink wine and look pretty.
They lived their lives free from trouble and care
And spent every morning combing their hair
They earned no money and these are the facts
They lived off the others who paid income tax.

As numbers continued to grow a problem occurred
A problem so great the like had never been heard.
In a factory built for mass producing oak Barrels
They now employed two hundred and twenty two Carols.
One hundred Celias and fifty seven called Elaine
A problem that even the Ken's could never explain.

It was a problem so great with no one to blame
For every Carol looked exactly the same.
It was the same with Celia, Denise and Elaine
All the girls were pretty and no one was plain.
The men were the same and that was not on.

How can you choose from two hundred men called Ron.

When a name was called out to go and see the boss
Hundreds turned up and he was always so cross.
The easy answer was their names had to change
But no other name was allowed in that land so strange.
It was written in laws from the beginning of time
That seven names only could be used in the land of Sunshine.

Production dropped and it was far from funny
For Ken their new boss lost a shed load of money.
Then Ken grew angry and threatened the sack
When the problem was solved by putting a number on their back.
When a person was called to partake of a brew
The Tannoy called our come in Carol one hundred forty two.

The land called Sunshine was again happy and pleased
And a new industry emerged through an Idea by a Denise.
It was started overnight by a Brian, Elaine and Ron
Who made one off tee shirts with names and numbers on.
Wedding vows also changed to bring an end to all strife
Do you Ken 92 take Celia 27 to be your dearly beloved wife?

Where the Pooch tree grows

In a far off land where the pooch tree grows
Live a tribe of giants with fifteen big toes.
They live off the fruit of this abundant tree
And with its wood made ships that sail on the sea.
The tree grows so tall and can be seen for miles
From Greenland's shores to the Canary Isles.
So useful was this resilient wood
Many came to cut it if only they could.

But the residents of the land were far from barmy
And twenty foot giants form an invincible army.

The loggers gave up and because of their greed
Were sentenced for life the giants to feed.
The trees are still there and it will always be so
For the giants secret weapon was a massive big toe.
So if you visit this land to look at these trees
You'll only come up to the youngest giant's knees.

Show them respect and if you're very good
They'll send you back home with a sample of wood.
But only a sample not a trunk, plank or even some fruit
For the multi toed giants have learned how to shoot.
In a far off land where the pooch tree grows
Live a tribe of giants with fifteen big toes.
Times for them has changed and no one needs their boats.
So they weave bark from the Pooch tree into fine winter coats.

Married Bliss

My friend's house is a place I like to go
To hear the latest news all the things I need to know.
But I often have a problem and a decision which to make
Just whose side in an argument tonight I will have to take.
Then Celia said, you'll never believe what Ken has done today
Is something I'm quite accustomed to and expect to hear her say.

I've had another bad day and feeling out of sorts
And Ken has done nothing to help me I regret I have to report.
I've vacuumed the carpets you can't deny that I've done that,
What! She cried out with a yell, all you've done is the back door mat.

Not knowing what to say I gave her a knowing smile,
It must be the cleanest doormat that I've seen for quite a while.

That's not all he's done she said with emotion and strong feeling,
He decided to fill that crack today in the middle of the ceiling.
That's good said I, you must be happy that he's doing the job at last,
She stared at me and then at Ken and her expression was aghast.
Happy, said Celia, he's useless; he's nothing but a joke
Without covering the carpets and settee what's a matter with the bloke.

I tried to point out Ken's good points to ease the atmosphere
But it would be easier learning Russian, I must get out of here.
Now Kenneth in his wisdom went to put the kettle on
And in the lounge sat Celia looking daggers across at Ron.
He tries his best, does Ken, said I with my tongue in my cheek
He must have done something right at some time during this week.

I did the shopping yesterday said Ken whilst carrying cups and biscuit jar
Shopping said she, you dropped me of at Morrison's and never left the car.
While we had our refreshments Celia's mood lightened up a lot
And as we talked about her paintings the happier she got.
I'll make some picture frames tomorrow said Ken who now sat on the floor
It was then I made my swift exit out of their wooden back door.

The Walking Group

The walking group meets every week
And set out from the local church.
Past rows of houses and into fields
Past mighty oaks and silver birch
Natures wonders for to seek.

Through woods and fields we boldly go
In summer sun and winter snow.
Tony in front and Karen behind
And other walk leaders of every kind
Walking for pleasure, bringing peace of mind.

A lively group of like minded friends
The lively chatter as they walk along.
Through countryside they wander on
See squirrels at play and birds at song

The joy they feel should never end.

To bird sanctuary or country park
This motley crew by car embark.
Along footpaths by canal and stream
To reservoir and sculpture park
And stop for tea or Walls' ice cream.

The benefits to health are great
A fact we often celebrate.
To see natures wonders as we walk
Through fields and woods or Barker's Park
We all agree we're glad to be
The walking group of Kimbewworth Park.

Cherry Wine and a Gladstone Bag

I used to have a Gladstone bag in which to keep my tools
I bought it from a Yorkshire lass, who used to teach in schools.
I met her while on a camping holiday which simply was divine
She was with a friend called Alice and they were drunk on cherry wine.

She stumbled across the campsite with her legs all wobbly and bent
And she tripped over a guy rope and fell into the warden's tent.
The lantern fell on the ground and the centre pole did sag
She fell over backwards upon her Gladstone bag.

She said her bag was too heavy and had caused her embarrassing fall
But if you knew that wicked lady you would not believe that at all.
She sold the Gladstone bag next day to a sober man named Ron

Ronald Town

To keep his bits and pieces in, in safety, from that sad day on.

Her friend called Alice was also drunk on cherry wine just then,
She was famous throughout Yorkshire for sketching naked men.
Back at the tent she spied poor Ron and gave him such a fright,
"I'm sleeping with my clothes on" he said, "You're not drawing me tonight".

The rest of my holiday simply was eventful to say the very least.
To drink bottles of cherry wine with fish and chips certainly was a feast.
The two ladies became the best of friends and I know this may be a shock
They drink coffee with my wife and I each week at one O'clock.

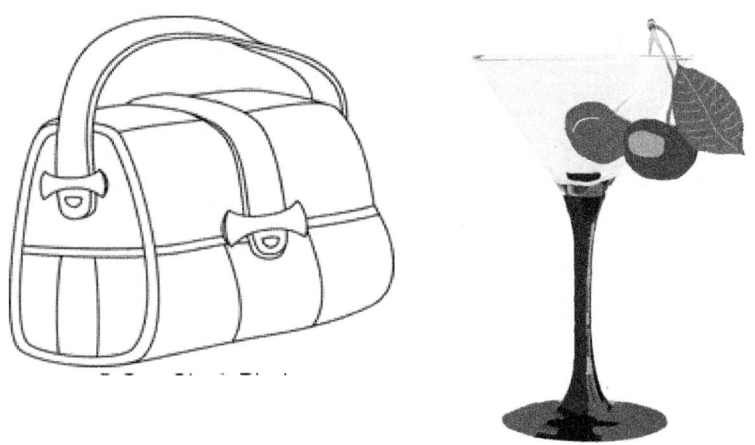

The Lost World of Wassa Matta And Others

Nonsense and serious poems
And silly short stories
By a Yorkshire man with a
weird sense of humour

Copyright © 2018

Ronald Town

Ronald Town

<u>In Memory Of</u>

Sue Mason

A good friend
And a lovely caring lady

Contents

Joy and peace

A tribute to David Barnes (Barney)

The magic carpet

My ten pet hates

My Viking inheritance

The church tea rota

The trauma of shopping

Short of money in old age

My first car

Thermal underwear

The wishing well

The exiled cricketer

Our grass is real

Over indulgence

My jumper of Lincoln green

My Sunday's in the fifties

Kimberworth Park in the early days

Not cabbage again mum

Wassa Matta again

I am an avid reader

When heaven revealed its glory

The Yorkshire lass at Derby Uni

A delegate in the making

The little sister

Why do pigeons nod their heads?

My bright blue spoon

The parallel Rons

The sea

The butcher's shop on St. John's Green

When I Were a Lad

Put that game away son, and go out and play,
You'll get square eyes watching that screen,
As my mother used to say.
But I'm on level sixty dad, and beating my best mate,
And playing out of doors is something that I hate.
When do you ever speak to people, that are not on a phone?
I spoke to some just last week, to Simon and to Joan.

Summer holidays are times for long walks in the woods
And for climbing up tall trees,
No chance, I don't like stinging nettles, and getting stung by bees.
Now listen to what I'm saying, because playing out is not all that bad.
I'll tell you what we used to do, when I were just a lad.

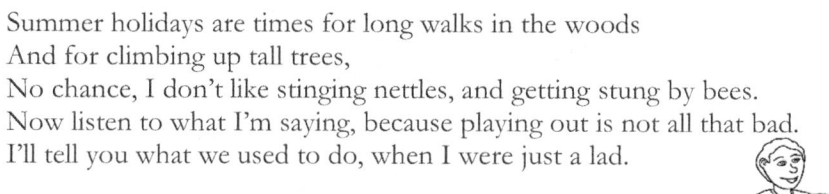

When we came home from school or at weekends
We were out on our bike.
We'd cycle out to Wentworth and any where we like.
Or walk around Greasbrough Dams with Ron, Les and Dave,
And stay in Scholes wood till it was dark, and pretend to be brave.
We'd play with bows and arrows and make a secret den,
And take our younger brothers there, Dennis, Barry and Ken.

At home we'd play with marbles, whip and tops and sledges,
Or we'd play at hide and seek behind our neighbours hedges.
At holiday time we'd spend all day in the fields and in the wood,
With our brothers, sisters and neighbours and life it would be good.
We'd take a bottle of water, and some jam sandwiches for our lunch.
We'd climb trees and run about, we were a merry bunch.

Sometimes after school we'd catch a bus to Masbrough station
With my train spotting mates
We'd see Scots and Brits and Jubilees, black fives 8Fs and Pates.
We'd often play football in the park, and sometimes on the green.
To see us in our fifties shorts was something to be seen.
So Peter, son, put away that X Box and get outside and play,
And save those stupid games of yours for the next rainy day.
(Brits is short for the Britannia class loco and Pates for the Patriot Class)

The Fair is Coming
(The Statutes fair was known locally and the Stattis Fair)

The fair is coming, said this kid at school,
Eric Brady was his name, and Eric was no fool.
It's called the Stattis said Jack Jones, another special mate,
This conversation had taken place, as we passed through the school gate.

Ralph O'Brian, a brainy kid of almost eleven,
Said "there's been a fair in Rotherham since 1207".
David Platts a pal of mine who was always in the know,
Said 1207, that's impossible mate, that's only four hours ago.

Walking home from school, on that cold October day,
Our thoughts were on that special event, just one month away.
A month's a long time to a ten year old kid,
But when the day finally arrived and here's what we did.

We were on the bus at half past five,
In days before I learned to drive.
On the bus we had two pence to pay,
And everyone on that bus, was going to the fair that day.

In mid-November come rain or shine,
We'd visit the fair from six o'clock till nine.
The Stattis was an annual treat,
And friends and family there would meet.

With brothers, sister, mum and dad,
We're going to the fair that can't be bad.
We've saved up for months and we've a bob or two,
For sweet candy floss, and hot dogs too.

Crowds of people you can see them smile,
On hearing the fair, from almost half a mile.
Loud music and screaming as we walked to the ground,
Came from roundabouts, spinning all around.

Dad handed out my money, which caused me to frown,
I'd saved up five bob and he gave me half a crown,

With a smile on his face and he gave me another,
And off I went quickly with Leslie my brother.

Come along now and try your luck,
At roll a penny, throwing darts and of course hook a duck.
We were having none of that, they were mere trifles,
We'd come to the fair to go on the rifles.

We spent two shillings, and had so much fun,
And we both agreed then to save up for a gun.
We went on the dodgems wearing funny hats,
And were chased around, by our friend David Platts.

We played at darts and other fairground stuff,
Before we agreed that we'd both had enough.
We decided then our parents we'd meet,
And buy a bottle of pop and something to eat.

With hot dogs and chips, our bellies did swell,
And candy floss after, left us feeling unwell.
We'd spent all our money and made such a fuss,
It's bedtime for you kids, said mum, we'll go catch the bus.

The fair is now over and the weather looks bleak,
Then we remembered its Christmas in just six week.

*In the year (1207AD) a fair was granted at Rotherham to last two days,
on the Vigil and Feast of St Edmund, 15th and 16th November.*

My best ever Christmas presents

Every Christmas I got football kits like other kids on my street.
What was Santa thinking of, for a kid with two left feet?
I wore the kit on Christmas day, while kicking my ball upon the green,
It was hidden in my wardrobe on Boxing Day, and never again to be seen.
I never liked playing football, which my mates thought quite weird.
And if I ever meet that Santa Clause I'm going to pull upon his beard.

But one Christmas I had a Meccano set, which was a young boys dream,
I was as happy as a pig in muck, or a cat that got the cream.
I made cranes and trains all day long I never wanted to stop,

I added to my set each week at Cooper's toy shop.
This was my favourite for many years, an iconic fifties toy,
Daddy Santa got it right for once, it was my pride and joy.
In nineteen fifty eight, my dad asked me, what would I like,
For Christmas in my eleventh year it had to be a bike.
On Christmas Eve I searched the house but nothing could be seen,
But on Christmas morning, there it was where could it have been?
Bikes were special things back then, the transport of the time,
I rode far and wide with my mates, in happiness sublime.

In nineteen hundred and sixty one I received my favourite gift,
A Stanley tool kit of my very own, almost too heavy for me to lift.
I used it in my garden shed, whenever I was free,
For woodwork was my passion, I was as happy as can be.
On September third the following year, I started work that day,
And my kit of tools has served me well, and I still use them to this day.

Over the years I've had many gifts like shirts and jumpers too,
Metal detectors and painting stuff just to name a few.
I've had a Samsung tablet and many other things,
I've collected stamps and tea cards and even balls of string.
I've had books by the dozen, tools and a fountain pen,
But I will never regain the excitement a young boy felt back then

The Lost World of Wassa Matta

The Beginning

In a time before remembering in a wooden building on a piece of fertile land
that in the distant future would become the deer park on the Wentworth
estate, known a Kimberworth Park, there lived two extraordinary men.
Ronnie Matta and Ken Wassa.

At a time in ancient history, a generation after men and women who wore
simple animal skins had left their caves, Ronnie and Ken were among the first
generation of farmers and lived in what became known as the Bronze Age. So
why were they extraordinary? It seemed that by some quirk of nature their
IQ was far beyond what would develop in Homo Sapiens in the next 4,000
years.

Ronnie and Ken's families had lived together for generations, and when in their early teens they developed a type of bronze that is now lost to the world. They made tools so sharp that their woodworking skills allowed them to make wooden dwellings of such exceptional quality, that people came from miles around to see them.

They invented the first kiln and used seasoned oak and ash to make furniture that was a delight to behold. They developed paper from wood and studied geometry and mathematics and dreamed of things that would not come into fruition for another four thousand years.

They invented the wheel at fifteen years of age and made a cart that could be pulled by an early form of horse.

One day Ken said to Ronnie "why don't we see what lies beyond this land in which we live?"

So after saying goodbye to their families they set off on their travels and after many weeks arrived on the beach of a great sea.

Ronnie said to Ken "let us make a craft that will allow us to travel over the water."

So with the tools that they brought with them they made what was possibly the first boat in history.

They were twenty years of age when this three storey vessel was completed. In the 21st century they would be acclaimed a young genius's. But these were two modest young men.

They had many adventures and eventually landed in a far off land and in a far off desert whilst digging for fresh water, discovered an underground world, made up of an immense cave system, containing vegetation and every known mineral. Thus the land of Wassa Matta began. They were also visited by two of their descendants in a time machine which we will hear about another time.

6000 later, Sometime in the late 20th Century

(The story of a descendant of Ronnie Matta called Ron)

In my early life I was a joiner on the film sets of Pinewood Studios and was discovered one day whilst fixing shelves in Jane Fonda's dressing room. She mistook me for the stand in or look –alike for Clint Eastwood, and begged me to star with her in the remake of the film, Robin of Sherwood and his Byrley Road Merry Men. Clint and I became friends when I modeled Saville Row suits for him over the years owing to my slim figure. I was also featured in his autobiography "Ron and Me".

Not wanting to pursue a career as an actor, due to my propensity to keep out of the limelight, Jane introduced me to a top modeling agency that were looking for someone to be the new face of Ivory cosmetics for very macho men. Of course I was perfect for the Job.

The headlines that week in the Rotherham Advertiser were *"Local wood man makes good man"*.

So ends the story of the early years of my life.

After thirty years of being a male model and fashion guru among the jet set in our capital city. I now decided that a change of lifestyle was in order. I was now a multi-billionaire and duly sold my penthouse flat in Mayfair, gave my pet giraffe to a friend at London Zoo and gave my extensive, expensive wardrobe to the Millwood home for retired poorly dressed vicars in Darnall and headed for the border between Iraq and Saudi Arabia to dig for the ancient lost city of Wassa Matta.

To accomplish this, I hired a range Rover; three camels, fifty local miners and a JCB and a metal detector.

I also hired a construction crew to build a hotel, general store; a fish and chip shop and a swimming pool. I only needed to buy cement and bricks for there was plenty of sand already there. The water came from an Oasis which also happened to be handy. The Oasis was also surrounded by fish ponds and potato fields which were handy for the fish and chip shop.

After settling in to my new lifestyle I studied a map of the hidden city of Wassa Matta which I had bought from a strange man called Ken Wia at a local flea market in Rotherham where I had also bought my giraffe and polar bear Snowy. The polar bear sadly died while crossing a busy London Road. He had forgotten to wait for the green flashing man as he had been taught to do.

One month after my new hotel was completed and after a hearty meal of fish and chips, guided by the map, we started to excavate with the JCB and on the second day, just after afternoon tea, at thirty feet down we struck a flat hard surface which turned out to be a landing above a stone staircase. At that moment which I will never forget, I knew just how Howard Carter must have felt on discovering the entrance to Tutankhamen's Tomb. That night we celebrated until the early hours and I treated my crew to pints of real ale and fish and chips.

We reached the bottom of the stone staircase after ten day's digging by hand. The staircase was seventy feet deep and in front of us was a door of solid gold with an inscription on the top edge which when translated from an ancient lost script said. This is the Secret entrance to the lost city of Wassa Matta. That was our first real clue that we were on the right track.

Fortunately for us, the door was not locked and when we opened the door we saw wonders beyond our wildest imagination. In front of us was an underground railway station complete with four sets of railway lines, buffet and Chinese take away. We later found out that the railway was 4300 miles long and came out in Shanghai, CHINA.

We approached the station master who was surprised to see us. He explained that the railway had been built by ancient Wassa Mattapeans who secretly invented the steam locomotive 3000 years before George Stevenson and built this first of many stations that we saw before us now.
The Wassa Mattapeons were famed throughout this world for their tunnelling skills and got so carried away that their descendants carried on digging for the next 3000 years and built a secret exit door in Shanghai.

I asked him the obvious question. Where did they dispose of all that stone, rock and other waste material?
On reflection his answer was obvious. Who do you think built the pyramids and the Great Wall of China he said?
As luck had it we had just arrived for the opening ceremony as the tunnel was completed that very day. Fate had intended us to be there.
A bottle of vintage Wassa Matta wine was to be broken on the side of a newly built steam engine built for the occasion. The name of the engine was Wassa Matta Choo Choo named after their new leader Barry Choo Choo's wife Chatta nooga Choo Choo.

We were told that during their excavations over the millennia they had discovered every known mineral and type of plant and were self-sufficient. They had secret exits all along the route to China from which the steam and smoke from the engines was removed.
The Wassa Mattapeons were short of nothing except one thing. Real Fish and Chips.

We immediately dispatched our miners and very soon they returned with five hundred portions of fish and chips complete with salt and vinegar and wrapped in the Wassa Matta Times newspaper.

They ate the food with gusto and could be heard chanting "there's only one Harry Ramsden", many miles away. They were so happy that from that day forward the King became known as Harry instead of Barry in memory of that great fish and chip man.

We lived with these wonderful people for three whole years and learned many things from each other.
We discovered long lost arts of working metal and wood and driving express trains and I in turn taught them how to become successful fashion models and how to tame and house train a giraffe and polar bear. Ken a friend who accompanied me from England taught them the art of using a scroll saw and making model farm houses for use in their nurseries and play groups.

We discovered that these people often came in to our world and travelled extensively and that one man called Ken Wia even visited Yorkshire and that his name had entered into the Yorkshire language. His tribal name was Wassa Matta wia. I then remembered that he was the very man who had sold me the map in Rotherham and sold me the giraffe and polar bear many years before. Ken Wia somehow knew that I was related to the original Ronnie Matta and that my friend Ken was related to the original Ken Wassa. How they knew they never revealed to us.
We were indeed destined to be the very ones to discover this underground wonderland.

Whilst in Rotherham Ken Wia had met and Married a beautiful Yorkshire girl working at the Kimberworth Co-op by the unusual name of Odea Rimee and after her marriage she was known locally as Odea Wassa Matta Wia.
By the time of our departure from Wassa Matta, steam railway trips were being launched from Shanghai to the Ron Town fish and chip shop and modelling agency on the border between Iraq and Saudi Arabia.

We sold the golden door to Fort Knox at a decent discount and with the money extended the railway line to Rotherham in South Yorkshire. The secret entrance came out under the studio of a painter of Chinese ladies in Rotherham. The neighbours soon got used to strange men and women carrying bags of chips walking up and down their drive at all times of day or night. Also Chinese Ladies came as models to that now famous art studio. The artist and her very knowledgeable husband, who just happened to my friend Ken, made a fortune from their new tea room and the back of the studio.

Five years later Yorkshire accents could be heard throughout Wassa Matta and at my chippie where many of my friends and Ken and Odea Wia served the best fish and chips in the world and were famous for their paintings of giraffes, polar bears, robins and Chinese ladies.

Later along with my friend Ken, whom I knew from my early days in Rotherham, and who according to Ken Wia was a descendant of Ken Wassa, invented a time machine and we visited our ancestors, Ronnie Matta and Ken Wassa during their stay in Wassa Matta. But that is another story.

Dreams of Sherwood

In a dream one night I was walking, down a path in fair Scholes wood,
I had travelled back in time it seemed, and stood there facing Robin Hood.
He was tall and slim, as any man that I have ever seen.
He had a longbow and quiver on his back, and was dressed in Lincoln green.

I asked him why he was in this wood, so far from his Sherwood den,
He said he was on a recruitment drive, and was looking for merry men.
I said I'd love to join him, but things were not as they seem,
I was fast asleep in bed I said, and had appeared to him in a dream.

He laughed at this and said to me,
You're really here with me, in this ancient wood,
You may remember, that you often made a wish, to meet with Robin Hood
These wishes were the magic words that drew you to our attention,
And in an instant you travelled here, to this fairy tale dimension.

With a click of his fingers we disappeared, and left the wood just then,
And landed in fair Sherwood, and I joined the merry men.
With a longbow at my shoulder's and a belt about my hips,
I had my first real meal with them, of venison and chips.

I became a famous archer and travelled far and wide,
Righting wrongs all round Nottingham with Robin by my side.
I believed things could not get better, than living in that wood,
Until waking up one morning, standing there was Robin Hood.

It's time to go back home he said, your dreams are at an end,
Your hedges are now overgrown, and the hedge cutters you need to mend.
Who was responsible, for ending this amazing idyllic life,
Who could possibly stop me enjoying myself;
It can only be the wishes of my wife.

So I landed back in Kimberworth, all the wiser for my adventure,
When I told my good friend Ken where I'd been,
He thought I'd got dementia.
So I kept the experience to myself, but the truth I really know,
For in my bed that very night,
I found six arrows and a great big wooden bow.

Fine with isolated showers

(The walking for pleasure group on a wet day)

We leave the church exactly on ten,
Around forty happy women and men.
Off on our walk and into the unknown,
Risk assessment done and whistle is blown.
We walk merrily through Barker's Park,
Chatting with friends as we walk.
The sun is shining and all is well,
Down through the Grange,
Heading for Dropping Well

At Thundercliffe Grange we stop and wait for Ron,
And have a jelly or humbug, but only take one.
That long winding path seems to go on forever,
We've travelled along in all kinds of weather.
We now realise the weather forecast was wrong,
It starts to rain before too long.
With water dripping down the back of our neck,
We've had a good walk so what the heck.

Along Hungerhill Road and turn left up that steep path,
The wettest we've been since we last had a bath.
Over the playing fields slowly we trudge,
Our shoes and our trousers all covered in sludge,
Tony's to blame we all shout together,
And Ron should have put a good word in,
About this blooming weather.
Now down the path past the Chislett Centre we slog,
Avoiding messy droppings left by some dog.

Whatever the weather we always have fun,
Now it's back to church for a cuppa, a biscuit or maybe a bun,
Announcements are made to those in the hall,
While Tony charges 20p for a go on spot the ball.
Breda's won again it's a fiddle it's a mistake,
Amidst jeers and shouting Breda chokes on her cake.
We're now as happy as Larry, you'll hear us all remark,
Cos we're the walking for pleasure group, on Kimberworth Park.

My Friend Sheila

Sheila Morely she's been poorly
But now she's feeling fine.
She's started training for charity walks
And drinking sparkling wine.

She's tried her hand at many things,
From woodwork to flying planes.
You may often find her jogging,
Down pleasant country lanes.

She's very good at craftwork,
And walking on hot coals.
And don't be surprised to see her
In the park and scoring goals.

She is a local hero
And always on the go.
She was quite an attraction
At the local Rotherham Show.

She juggled knives and boiled eggs,
Whilst standing on a bed,
The eggs came down in slices,
Upon two lumps of bread.

She's now famous throughout the borough
And in Scunthorpe Town too.
And if you want to get her autograph,
You'll have to join the queue.

Sheila Morely she's been poorly,
Now she is much better,
And after reading my silly poem,
She'll be writing me a letter.

Bluebells in Spring

(Another walking group saga)

Woolley woods in springtime
A walk not far from home.
A group of Kimberworth Park walkers
Through Woolley woods did roam.

Now Woolley woods in May time, is the place to be.
For a myriad of bluebells is a sight to see.
There was Colin with his Nikon taking pictures everywhere,
Attracting a crowd of locals who at the camera they did stare.

The friends marched on undaunted
Taking in that wondrous sight.,
What a wonderful Wednesday morning,
When the sun was shining bright.

Now Chris espied a hillock
And climbed to the very top.
And coming down his speed increased,
And with great difficulty came to a stop.
Next up the hill was Tony,
Who came down the hill with grace.
Closely followed by Ron ,
Who fell flat upon his face.

Karen, not wanting to be beaten,
And at the top she raised her thumb.
And laughing tripped over a tree root,
And landed on her bum.

Now the walk continued for an hour,
And a sweetie stop they did take.
This was not enough for our Marian,
Who ate a piece of chocolate cake.

The group began singing marching songs
And their voices made quite a din.
But the locals liked he sound they made,
And went round with a collecting tin.

Now if you go to the woods in May time,
Climbing hillocks you should not choose.
Or you'll end up like our Karen,
With a midge bite on your ankle,
And on your bum a bruise.

Fruit of the Land
(A Harvest Poem)

Bramley apples on trees so tall,
Pears growing against the garden wall.
Cherries, plums and greengage too,
Damsons and figs to name a few.
Can all be grown in our British soil
By God's provision and human toil.

Fruit from abroad we eat each day,
Bananas and passion fruit from far away.
Kiwi and melon, orange and grape,
Lemons and Mangoes from the far off cape.
Guavas and quince, Passion fruit are fun,
Matured in South American sun.

Blackberries and raspberries smaller in size,
Eaten by themselves or baked into pies.

Loganberries and Worcester berries and red current too,
Tayberries and Joster berries and berries so blue.
Gooseberries prickly made into a crumble,
But top of my list are strawberries so humble.

From a global perspective its harvest all year round
In shops and markets all this produce is found.
Seed sown by farmer and gardeners in spring of each year,
Wheat for our bread and hops for our beer.
Apples from Kent and cider from Devon,
Seen by our Creator God in his heaven.

It matters not which fruit we seek,
They are available now in our shops each week.
Fruit, vegetables and grain God's gift to mankind,
A wonderful variety in shops and gardens we find.
We can be thankful for them all and be of good cheer,
As we celebrate at our harvest festival once again this year.

Every day is special

There are quite a number of special times in the average year,
Christmas Day is my favourite but it's over far too quickly I fear
Ordinary days can become very special to me and also to some of you,
Times when I am painting with my friends and enjoying what I do.

To enjoy these pleasures, you do not have to be a rich man or a king
Or only enjoy the pursuits, that such great wealth can bring.
Just being together enjoying like interests and maybe having fun,
Designing craftwork with a friend over a cup of tea and a bun.

Creative writing and other things ,with like-minded people, can also be
A special time, a happy time, like a day trip to the sea.
Days of summer long and warm, as in woods and fields with friends we roam,
And after a long and joyous time, it's also special to come home.

Special times can be every day, at work at play or prayer,
All is needed is special people, with whom our life we share.
There are perfect days in life, and quickly they are gone,
We keep them in our memories, long after the day is gone.
We spend our lives looking forward, to this or that special time, but why?

Let's make today that special time, we can do it if we try.

In My Dreams

I have lived on planet earth for over seventy years,
And I've had my ups and downs, and have shed so many tears.
And in my distant youth, I'll admit I was much fitter,
I started work at fifteen making John Smith Bitter.

At eighteen I got the sack, for drinking on the job,
I couldn't afford to drink in pubs, for I only earned five bob.
At twenty one I became a joiner, and worked on local schools,
Using a Christmas gift from mum and dad, a set of woodwork tools.

At twenty five I left that job, for the work it was too hard,
And went to work for a very nice man, who owned a breakers yard.
My job was to watch the customers, and stop them nicking parts,
There were all kinds of vehicles there, including ice cream carts.

At twenty seven I was married, and decided to settle down,
And I went back to be a Joiner, in good old Rotherham Town.
At thirty, I learned to fly a plane, and flew to Istanbul,
I ate too much local food, and my belly was quite full.

I sold my plane and bought a car, bright yellow with shiny chrome,
Because it matched the curtains, in the front room of my home.
At fifty I became an actor, and played in Summer Wine for a laugh,
I was the man who cleaned a car, next door to Ivy's Caff.

At sixty I retired and concentrated on my looks,
I found that this was a waste of time, so I wrote some poetry books.

Time Travel in 1752 England

A short story

It was a sunny afternoon in late autumn of 1752 when 17 year old Rosie Byrley left her thatched cottage or keeper's Lodge as it was known locally in the Kimberworth Deer Park to visit her aunt Bessie in the small hamlet of Scholes. She passed herds of fallow deer and red deer and in the distance she saw her father with his longbow drawn and looking towards a group of rabbits on a grassy bank about fifty yards away. Hey up dad shouted Rosie "I'm fed up with rabbit for supper, can't we have venison for a change." "What and lose my job," her father replied. His employer Charles Watson Wentworth Earl Fitzwilliam and also prime minister allowed him three deer a year as part of his wage as game keeper and woodsman on the Wentworth estate. "Go about yer business" said her father, "you've scared the rabbits off now, happen we'll have nowt for supper tonight and yer mum won't be pleased when I tell her it were your fault." "Maybe I'll catch a couple of birds if I'm lucky," said her father. In reality her father could not hit a barn door with a frying pan and only fired at groups of rabbits hoping to hit one of them. He would only hit a bird if he was aiming in another direction.

Rosie and her father both laughed and Rosie hugged her father and continued towards Scholes Coppice.
In the 1700s the coppice covered a large area and almost reached Greasbrough village.
Rosie strolled through the woods watching the foxes and rabbits and all manner of birds and suddenly out of nowhere a strange woman suddenly appeared. She was wearing clothes unlike any that Rosie had ever seen before. They were made of bright coloured material and on her feet were beautiful red shoes.
"Hey up" said Rosie in her broad Yorkshire accent "where did you get them weird clothes from?"
"Come with me and I'll show you" said the lady who told Rosie that her name was Tracey Stirling.
She led Rosie behind a great oak tree and in to a shiny silver sphere and introduced her to a tall man in even stranger clothes who said "hello, I'm Phillip Stirling. " Tracey helped Rosie to a seat and brought her a Cola. After a lifetime of stream water and watered down beer Rosie was overwhelmed at the taste of this strange drink. When she had composed herself she asked the obvious question. "Who are you?" "We're time travellers" said Phillip. "And this is our time machine."

"I'm 600 years old and from a planet in the sky and married a woman from Earth" said Phillip "I'm from your world and I've come from two hundred and seventy five years in your future said Tracey." "Would you like to see what it is like in the year 2017 said Phillip?" "My aunt will be worried if I am late said Rosie." "This is a time machine and we can get you back to your aunts before and time has passed," said Phillip. Rosie knew that she should not go with strange people but somehow she trusted Tracey and her dad, Phillip.

A strange noise came from the middle of the Sphere and when the doors opened Rosie was in a wonderland. "Where am I said Rosie?" "In Rotherham town centre said Tracey" "But Rotherham has only a few buildings said Rosie." Then she saw the Parish Church and knew that they were right.

Phillip and Tracey took Rosie into a large supermarket and bought her a meal which was different than anything that she could ever imagine. They then filled a couple of trolleys with all kinds of food and of course 100 cans of Cola. They re-entered the Sphere and took her to modern day Kimberworth Park and the very spot where her house used to be was a row of houses behind the church. She was amazed that the street was named after her family and called Byrley Road.

She then visited the Chislett centre and met a group of even stranger people, the Creative Writing Group.

"What is that strange drink that weird group of people are drinking" said Rosie". "It's called tea said Tracey" and poured a cup out for Rosie with two sugars which she drank and savoured every mouthful. A lovely lady called Denise made her a chip buttie and she was almost in tears at the pleasure of tasting this national dish and in return taught Denise an eighteenth century folk song and dance which Denise now performs on Karaoke nights at her local pub, where she is the star attraction. She then sat with the creative writing group and told her wonderful story and spoke of life in her day. And of Good king George the second, new to the throne.

"An extremely intelligent looking man called Ron told Rosie that he had lived for twenty years in a house built on the very spot where she lived and he showed her a precious stone on a gold chain which he had dug up in the garden when planting prize his winning sprouts. Tears appeared in everyone's eyes as she tearfully spoke of losing this very item 250 years earlier. She smiled as Ron presented her with her long lost jewel.

Phillip invited the group to come with him to visit Clara's house and together they delivered all the wonderful food to Rosie's mum Hayley Byrley and the problem of supper was solved for many a day which was fortunate because Rosie's dad Walter Byrley had failed to shoot a rabbit for supper. Denise introduced Hayley to potatoes and chip making and gave her the bag of seed potatoes she had brought with her. Hayley promised to plant potatoes in the spring.

They then went and met Rosie's dad Walter and Ron and his extremely intelligent friend Ken gave him some tips on how to fire a bow and arrow correctly and gave him two balls of string which they just happened to have with them at the time. He eventually became the champion archer of all England and never forgot the two skilled and intelligent men who taught him to shoot and so much more besides.

Ron also gave him one of his three penknives. He was so grateful that he named his keeper's lodge Robinstown in honour of their visit.

They then dropped Rosie off at her aunts along with some food and Cola. Rosie's aunt Bessie Byrley was famous for inventing the Yorkshire pudding a fact which is now lost in the annals of time. Ken said "did you know that Aunt Bessie's Yorkshire puddings are now famous throughout the land in our time." This made her day and no one had the heart to tell her that it was named after some other aunt Bessie. "I have had a wonderful time" said Rosie. "Will you please come again?" "We'll visit you again at Christmas and bring you some special food and drink" said Phillip "on the understanding that you will tell no one of what you have seen." He said this for it may have changed history, for imagine what would happen if cola was invented 250 years too early. There would be no Coca Cola company and no Father Christmas.

He left them to eat the 21st century food and took the writing group back to the Chislett. Giving Dawn a shock as the Sphere landed in the kitchen and squashed the waste bin. Phillip replaced it with an even better one from the Sphere. The writing group then went back to their seats and surprisingly none of them could think what to write about that day. They then returned to their respective homes and cooked a meal of Aunt Bessie's Yorkshire pudding washed down with 18th century beer.

Ron and Ken were silently proud of themselves for training the champion archer of all England, who in turn taught future kings how to shoot.

Their wives deemed themselves very fortunate indeed to have such intelligent and talented husbands and were proud to wait on them hand and foot.

My Collections

I used to collect postage stamps, as many young men do,
I collected stamps from Switzerland, from Mexico and Timbuktu.
I bought many stamps from Woolworths, and would eagerly await,
For the postman on a Saturday coming through our garden gate.
Over time my interest waned, and I discovered things that I liked more,
And my albums were kept in a cardboard box, behind my wardrobe door.

Books replaced the stamps that were the joy in early life,
A passion that I share today, with my daughter and my wife.
I tried to catalogue my books one day, and didn't know where to start,
I have so many books on woodwork, and a hundred books on art.
I know I should resist them, but don't know how to stop.
So for every new book I collect today, one goes to the charity shop.

Old woodwork tools were a passion all my adult life,
I collected planes and chisels, and a rosewood marking knife.
I have a cupboard full of them, and one day I must get rid.
You can buy them all this afternoon, for about six hundred quid.
People today don't use them, what a pity and what a shame.
Power tools have replaced them, but the satisfaction's not the same.

Today my collections are much simpler, than they were back then,
I no longer collect tools and stamps, but the humble fountain pen.
I've got silver pens and black pens, and a couple that are red,
I get excited when I use them, I can't wait to get out of bed.
I write today in italics, as I did as I did at school, way back then,
And my enthusiasm is now catching; I've passed it on to Ken

People collect many strange things, from old spanners to garden gates,
I have a friend called Colin, who collects plastic cups and paper plates.
He has knives and forks, by the hundred and cereal bowls galore.
He cannot get around his house, for piles upon the floor.
He bought them for a bargain price, of one hundred and fifty for a pound,
He now has enough paper plates, to cover a football ground.

He can't find his beloved cameras for his many piles of plates,
An impossible situation which our Colin surely hates.
At last he sees his Nikons, beyond his Moorcroft Jugs,
Behind four hundred dinner plates, and five hundred plastic mugs.
How can I possibly get rid of these mugs, plates, knives and forks and all?

I'll use them at the harvest supper in St. John's, church hall.

A Painter and Poet's Dream
A short Story

I had waited many years for this day, the day when my dreams of being recognised as a painter and poet of comical verse came to fruition. Today I was to meet the foremost writer, poet and painter of this generation and was still overwhelmed that she had agreed to read my four volume book of poetry and nonsense short stories entitled Wassa Matter meets the Byrley Road merry men at an exhibition of my work at the Chislett Creative Art Gallery in Rotherham.

Lady Mary Faifax Gladys Smedley was renown throughout the world for her work in the genre of Cornish poetry and Chinese painting and was well known for her generosity in launching the careers of many of today's celebrated artists and poets. Well known names such as Cheesy Grumble, Wayne Dribble and Sonya Orchard to name a few.

I first came to her attention when she read my poem, The Byrley Road Merry Men in this year's publication of The Yorkshire Eskimo, and obtained my address from the publishers. I received her letter on the Monday morning and all that week I couldn't sleep for wondering if I would be the next poet who would benefit from her patronage and that of her husband Sir Hugh Montgomery Smedley the well-known formula one racing driver and painter of plywood giraffes, elephant rider and coconut Juggler. He came second on Britain's Got Talent to a polar bear wrestler when a coconut landed on a well known judge's head. Lady Mary had already launched the career of the Honourable Carol Jeffries Walsh the wealthy painter of cathedrals, litter bins and bus stops and maybe one day I too would become as famous as Carol and have Lady Mary as my patron and mix in such exalted circles?

As the hours ticked away to the visit to my humble exhibition, my mind went back many years to when it all began. It was a warm summer's day in the Yorkshire fishing resort of Whitby where I was on holiday with my family. I have always had an interest in painting and drawing and encouraged by aunt Elsie who lived in this wonderful place we visited a back street art shop by the name Le Pomme D'or. This shop which I visited many times over the coming years was an inspiring artist's dream and on this sunny August afternoon I bought my first sketch pad a 2B pencil, a small tin of watercolour paints and a packet of Spangles from Bungle's sweet shop next door,.

For the full fortnight in 1960 in one of those summers when the sun always seemed to shine, I sketched the famous Abbey whose origins go back to 657 AD and was founded by the first abbess Lady Hilda. I sketched St Mary's and St. Hilda's churches and that wonderful harbour. Every evening after supper I would sit in the conservatory in Love Lane and paint those wonderful buildings and views.

On the second afternoon, sitting on a bench near the famous whale bones a lovely lady came and sat down beside me. I offered her a Spangle, which she gratefully accepted, and she admired my work. During our conversation I discovered that she was a well-known local poet by the strange name of Doris Sybil Marble and as we met over the next few days she encouraged me to start writing about what I saw as I painted the local views.
Encouraged by Doris, I kept a journal and I naturally moved into the genre of monologues and comic verse.

In those idyllic years I visited Whitby many times and encouraged by Doris Marble, whom I often stayed with, I visited the local area and painted more of those wonderful North Yorkshire landscapes and wrote many poems on a variety of subjects and dreamed that one day I would be recognised as a painter Poet of Yorkshire, not realising that I would have to wait almost fifty years and that it would be the influence and encouragement of a local creative writing group that would set me on the path that would lead me to Lady Mary Faifax Gladys Smedley.

Doris lived to the ripe old age of 104 and sadly died on a Friday afternoon in May whilst eating a Spangle. Her funeral was attended by poets from throughout the UK. I had the great honour of reading my poem about Doris entitled "Don't Eat Spangles in May". Sadly Spangles are no longer available and I have now moved on to M & Ms.

At last the big day arrived and Lady Mary Faifax Gladys Smedley arrived on an elephant guided by her husband. She graciously gave my paintings and poetry her blessings and during that day I sold over five hundred books and all of my watercolour paintings. As she rode into the sunset on Bobbin the elephant I went home a happy and wealthier man. I owe everything that I am today to my wife, Lady Mary and of course Doris and Spangles.
The End

Vehicles

My favourite vehicle is by far,
Not a bus or tram or a racing car.
Not a bicycle, a coach, or a Vespa scooter
Or a vintage car, with big red hooter.
A hot air balloon with its skin all wet,
Nor a pedalo or gondola or a jumbo jet.
For none of these vehicles can ever compare,
To a steam locomotive of yesteryear.

Sir William Stanier designed a lot,
The Jubilees and the Royal Scot.
And Gresley locomotives to name a few,
The Mallard and the Flying Scotsman too.
Built at Doncaster's famous plant years ago,
A train spotter's haven and I should know.
Robert Riddles designed the Britannia's built at Crew,

Oliver Cromwell, Vulcan and Byron to name a few.

The smell of smoke and the hiss of steam,
Was the subject every young lad's recurring dream.
With, sandwiches and note book, pencil and combine too,
We were off to Doncaster, York or Crewe.
To fifties and sixties lads it was more than a game,
It was the excitement when underlining a brand new name.
I loved my bike and I love driving my car,
But a steam locomotive outshone them all by far.

The Peacock Painter from Barnsley

On the A629 near Barnsley, lies a medieval village,
That had such a reputation, even the Vikings didn't pillage
In AD 795 The Vikings came to Yorkshire and got as far as Lepton,
And raided the local Co-op, while all the people there just slept on.
They stocked up with groceries, as they began to invade our nation,
But they were turned back sixteen miles away, at a village with a reputation..

With broadsword and shield, they marched throughout that summer's day,
But fourteen miles from Lepton, a muster of peacocks blocked their way.
Four hundred savage peacocks, charged and flapped their wings in warning,
And chased the Vikings back to Lepton, on that historic Friday morning.
They ran as far as Blackpool, and sailed back home in fear,
And didn't come back to England for another thirty year.

Now the peacocks were happy, in that village once again,
They were lovingly cared for, by a painter girl called Jane.
She made a living painting peacocks, and at this she became adept.
But she also painted sunset scenes, while the four hundred peacocks slept.
You could often see her up on the hill, with her paint box and her easel.
Surrounded by sleeping peacocks, her guitar and Bernadette her weasel.

Now in every generation in that village, until the present day,
A lady called Jane paints her peacocks, and her acoustic guitar does play.
She paints peacocks and sunsets, in an art group with her friend Ron,
She copies them from her tablet, for the peacocks are long gone.
But still in Scandinavia, they sing of peacocks and Viking pillages,
And of Lady Jane the painter, in the most scary of Yorkshire villages.

Yellow Chalk

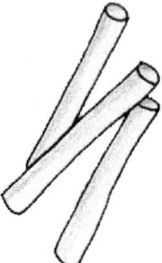

I have collected many things and people laugh at me.
I collected sticks of yellow chalk since the age of three.
Yellow is my favourite colour, and you never will believe,
That I have a bright red jumper, with a yellow sleeve.
I always wore black and white, from my early teens.
But my all-time favourite was a pair of yellow jeans.

My thousand sticks of yellow chalk is sadly now all gone,
It was stolen from my garden shed, by another lad called Ron.
It left a gaping hole in my life, which was difficult to fill,
Until I bought one thousand keys, from a kind old man called Bill.
I count my keys almost every day, and know them all by sight,
And if that Ron tries to steal them, with me he'll have to fight.

My latest collection was in the national news,
As the first person to collect one million screws.
Each week without exception, I count them in my shed,
And put them all in their proper place, before I go to bed
People round here think I'm sad, and completely off the rails,
But they'd have no doubt at all, if the caught me counting nails.

I also collect banana skins, and stick them on my wall,
Alongside my collection of orange peel and a punctured rugby ball.
My collections are so varied, and I'm famous on our street,

For no one else around me, has half a ton of luncheon meat
I'm also famous for my gloves, and I've two hundred and ninety one,
But my all-time love has got to be, my yellow chalk stolen by burglar Ron.

Get rid of that rubbish says my wife, especially that smelly banana skin.
And as for your tins of Luncheon meat, it's inside our wheelie bin.
The orange peel she said is next to go, onto our compost heap,
So if you collect banana skins or orange peel, I have some going very cheap.
My wife and daughter have just gone out, for their weekly morning walk,
So I can get at last on Amazon, to buy a thousand sticks of yellow chalk.

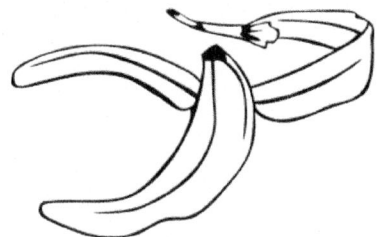

Winter

A frosted mass of the finest lace,
Adorn our hedgerows in this land.
Squirrels do our gardens grace,
Eat food left out by human hand.
All part of what winter's many joys can bring,
Making way for the wonders of the spring.

Snow decked hills and fields we see,
A carpet of white untouched by man.
A panorama as pure as pure can be,
All part of our God's perfect plan.
A wonderland throughout the day,
What joy to watch our children play.

Cold forgotten as we remember,
Fairy lights and that open fire.
Memories of some far off December,
Playing in fields all day and never tire.
The joy of another Christmas morn,
When Christ the king on earth was born.

As we walk through woods and fields,
Signs of hope does nature bring.
Buds appear, green shoots earth yields,

All wondrous signs of the coming spring.
Never wish away this dark cold season,
God gave us winter for a reason.

In wintertime all nature rests,
And flowers and trees all seem to die.
Birds of the air prepare their nests,
All natures wonders dormant lie.
But very soon the earth will ring,
With songs of joy for the long awaited Spring..

Train Spotting
(A Day at Doncaster Station)

We step off the train at Doncaster on a Thursday afternoon,
The spotters have already gathered, something must be coming soon.
Donny station at two thirty, Andy, Trevor and me,
Watching out for freight trains, is a pleasure for to see.

Gone are the days of steam, perhaps an occasional treat through here,
No more Deltics or other locos now, rarer than steam we often fear,
Doncaster is a favourite; it's good to be here once again
We now hear from platform three a cry, in the distance a freight train.

The spotters gather quickly round, with cameras and pens in hand,
Another one we've copped today, came a shout from within that merry band.
There are younger spotters around today, but many are as old as me,
Remnants of the steam age, the born again spotters are we.

People who speak our language, who recall those bygone spots.
Who remember streaks, A1s and Jubilees and of course the Royal Scots,
It's not out of sadness we meet here, its recapturing a simpler age.
Before X boxes and computer games, when conversation was all the rage.

People who see beauty in British workmanship, on trains both old and new,
From shiny brass parts, or painted works of art, just to name a few.
There's more than trains, to see at the station, there are many sights to see.
Police arresting people for being on the tracks, and the odd celebrity.

There are all types of people, getting on and off the trains each day.
Hen parties on their way to York or Brid, all in colourful array.

We sit and chat on a bench, in the summer sun, on a quiet afternoon
No trains running at the moment but there'll be something along quite soon.
It's time for a drink and a sandwich and we move over to platform one,
We are the modern train day spotters, Andy Trevor and Ron.

Every man must have his shed

I have a strange feeling that before I go to bed,
Somehow I'll have to escape to the safety of my shed.
No woman can every understand, why anyone ever would,
Want to spend so many hours, in a building made of wood.

It's man's answer, to prevent all those senseless, pointless rows,
It ought to be an addition, to all our wedding vows,
Which countless vicars ought to have said
Will you, love, honour and obey, and then go into your shed.

Sheds are useful for countless reasons, of which I will explain,
A man can keep his treasures there, which his wife thinks are a pain.
Tools, nails and screws, paint and bits of old cars,
Off cuts of wood and sandpaper, and many things in jars.

Old locks and window catches, all things that may come in handy,
Turpentine, glue and French polish, and a secret store of brandy.
How can men live without one, I wonder till this day?
It's a refuge from those household chores, I'll explain it if I may.

There's a crack in our ceiling, she said, so fill it now you must,
With proper filler this time, and not more putty I trust.
She'll keep on nagging at you, and it gets into your head,
So there's only one solution, spend some time within your shed.

You'll need a good excuse, to escape from your dear wife,
I know what to do; I'll go up to my shed, for my filler and filler knife.
I'll play with my nail gun, and offcuts of wood, until I get that innate feeling.
That she's forgotten all about that crack, in our front room ceiling.

To go to that refuge, is what every man must do,
And stay there and make things, till you're hungry, or have need for the loo.
It's a man's place; it's a sanctuary, a workshop and a bower,
So long as his dear wife brings him, a hot drink every hour.

It's too untidy for a woman, with wood and sawdust on the floor,
But to a man it's his special place, when he shuts the door.
With the divorce rate now so high, and no answer seems to be around,
A wife is contented in knowing, where her husband can be found.

The Door to Glory

Good Friday was the disciple's loss,
Their Saviour nailed upon a cross.
He seemed to be without a friend,
Betrayed and deserted at the end.

But that darkest day was meant to be,
Our saviour triumphed on that tree.
The carpenter turned that cross so gory,
Into the door that led to glory.

Disciples and friends all forlorn,
Met the Risen Lord on Easter Morn,
Oh what joy for tears of gladness,
Replaced the tears of heart rending sadness.

The Disappearing Milkman

Wally the milkman was as smooth as silk,
For forty odd years he delivered our milk.
Until that fateful day, when no sound came from his van,

And nothing was seen again, of that delivery man.
We asked our neighbours, what had happened to him.
We don't know a Wally, our milkman's called Jim.
No one else have ever heard of our Wally,
They started to think I was off my trolley.

Three months later pushing a Morrison's trolley,
Who should we see but our old milkman Wally.
Whilst standing near the semi skimmed shelf,
Our Wally turned into a fairy tale Elf.
He ran along to the pre-cooked meat pies,
And disappeared there right before our eyes.
We arrived home as shocked as can be,
To find elfin Wally sitting on our new settee.

Poor Wally was full of remorse and guilt,
As he spoke of a time before our house was built,
Beneath our house and this is no joke,
Was the invisible dwelling of all local fairy folk.
For elves to keep their mortality, and keep death at bay,
They had to visit their magical home, once every third day.
I had to do this said Wally, midst sobbing and tears.
By delivering two pints of green tops, for forty odd year.

To miss one day, I would slowly begin to become mortal,
And this would seal off, this magical Elfin portal.
On that fateful day, which ended my milk delivery game.
I was knocked down by a mini bus, and unconscious I became.
I woke up in hospital, and four days had gone by,
Making entry through the portal, impossible to try.
My magic milk float and green tops, had faded all away,
So I my own milk I buy from Morrisons,
And one pound a litre I now have to pay

We all felt sorry for Wally, this wonderful old feller,
So under our house we built, an amazingly huge cellar.
We excavated tons of rocks and soil and stone,
And finally exposed Wally's, magical ancestral home.
With an invisible entrance, behind our garden shed,
Our ex milkman Wally, could at last sleep in his own bed.
Over the years we met many, Elfin folk of that very same ilk
But we still had to go to Morrison's, to buy our semi skimmed milk.

The art group that saved my life

I decided on a Monday morning, that I would learn to paint,
I bought all the gear on Amazon at a price that made me faint.
The brushes cost me seventy pounds, and the easel fifty four,
The tubes and palette another sixty pounds, and the paper thirty more.
I bought a box to keep my stuff in, a water container that looked so quaint,
And after spending three hundred pounds, I didn't know how to paint.
When I went back on Amazon, it was my wife's turn now about to faint,
When I spent hundred pounds on books. to teach me how to paint.
 I tried to paint a woodland scene, with bluebells in cobalt blue,
It looked like a picture painted, by my daughter when she was only two.

You've spent all our savings said my wife, and you have the talent of our cat,
Go into the bedroom with this emulsion paint, and have a go with that.
I painted the ceiling in silence, with tears and paint now in my eyes,
And imagined myself painting landscapes,
With green fields and bright blue skies.
I forgot to put down dust sheets, and splashed shocking pink upon the floor,
And as my wife threw me out of the bedroom,
I saw I'd forgotten to paint the door.
For hours I pondered on my problems, as I sat on a bench in Barker's Park,
When a friend suggested I join an art group, at St. John's Kimberworth Park.

It was the solution to my problem, as I learned to paint there that very day,
New friends advised my how to paint, and only one pound for to pay.
Jane showed me techniques with my brushes, and Ron how to apply a wash,
At twelve O'clock we had a ten minute break, when we ate our nosh.
My paintings improved week by week, and a new painting style started when,
I was taught how to paint oriental ladies, by Celia and husband Ken.
I entered paintings in local art shows, which no one would have guessed,
And with the prize money paid back our savings,
And even my wife was impressed

OCD- Obsessive Cushion Disorder
(Celia's Lament)

I started collecting cushions, for no apparent reason,
I now have one hundred cushions, twenty five for every season

Cushions for the winter, for summer, autumn and spring,
I don't need a reason for doing this, for cushions is my thing.

When I change my curtains, I change my cushions too,
That's not obsessive behaviour, it's what arty people do.
My cushions are varied in colour, and subject matter too,
I even have a cushion, to match the seat in our loo.

I now have cushions to match every curtain, and this I must confess,
So I'm now collecting curtains, to match my daily dress.
I have striped dresses, and even some that are pink and frilly,
I am now getting aggro, because my husband thinks I'm silly.

But now I have a problem, which my husband pointed out,
I have counted fifty dresses; you'd better chuck some cushions out.
You've filled every wardrobe with cushions, you'd better buy no more,
This has got to be the last straw; all my clothes are on the floor.
I now realise that I am OCD, with four cushions on every bed,
But the answer came to me in a flash; we'll keep them in your shed

A Whistle Stop Tour

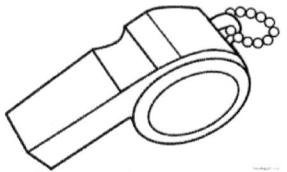

A short Story

On sunny afternoon in July I was walking through Scholes wood and out of the corner of my eye I saw a movement and to my amazement I saw a fairy about 18" high running past a small copse of ash saplings and she suddenly vanished right in front of me. I said to myself, "that's strange that is" and upon approaching the spot where she disappeared I saw something shining upon the ground and that was my first glimpse of the golden magic whistle that was to change my life for good.

I picked up the whistle and in an instant I was transported to a place I had often imagined in my wildest dreams, a land where the sun always shone and where I was once again young and slim. I looked around me and realised that I was invisible to everyone but myself and walked for hours in this magical wonderland and for nourishment I ate the fruit of the silver stemmed trees which tasted unlike anything that I had encountered before.

Just when I thought that I was unique I was approached by none other than my friend Ken who like myself had found his own magic whistle many years before and I suddenly knew the reason for his great knowledge. The air in this magical world was having an effect on me also and suddenly knew many things that I had not known before.

In that strange and wonderful land we made a pact that we would never disclose our secret to anyone not even our wives and that once a week in the early hours of the morning we would visit Fantastica as it became known to us. Ken informed me that if we blew our whistles again that we would be back where we started without any time having passed at all.

One sad thing about Fantastica was that you could bring nothing back with you only your magic whistle which once blown by a new owner become their property for life.

For many years a young Ron and Ken blew their whistles a five o'clock in the morning and wandered for hours around Fantastica and increased our knowledge on many subjects and back home became admired by our families who were proud to be related to two such knowledgeable men.

On our travels we learned a great deal about the land of fairies and silver fruit trees and I have written this today with Ken's agreement. We have not been to Fantastica for a few months because we are afraid of becoming so clever that people back home may become suspicious.

Then after a break of six months we once again visited Fantastica and discovered that by sucking on our whistle we became visible to the elven community.

We soon became known as the wise ones and hosted a new programme on the Elven and Pixie TV Channel called *If you don't know then we do* in which we were asked about many topics that had baffled the locals for centuries. Topics such as how to make a flower press and how to yodel in four languages.

In payment for our services we were given the secret of turning apple pies into gold which is very useful when faced with a glut of Bramley apples. We only did this once because one golden pie was worth 25 million pounds and how can you explain to the Inland Revenue where you obtained it.

We still go to Fantastica most days and please do not tell anyone what I have told you because they will come in a white van and take us both away.

Holiday Fated but Fun

(This was a true story and took place in July/August in 1972
whilst on holiday with Ron my next door neighbour)

Where shall we go on holiday? said two Ronnies from Rotherham,
So they drove up the Great North Road one Friday Night,
And got stuck in a traffic Jam.
That was only the start of their misfortunes,
On that ill fated Friday night in July,
They had to be towed off the A1 carriageway, I'll explain the reason why.

They pitched their tent in a scrap yard near famous Ferrybridge,
Next to a Morris Minor, a scooter, a pram and a fridge.
With their car with the faulty clutch, parked by the ridge tent's side,
The scrap yard was locked till Saturday morning,
With two Ronnie's locked inside,

The Viva was fixed by mid morning,
And most of their holiday cash was now spent,
They passed through Appleby by teatime,
And at Kitkby Thore pitched their tent.

Dressed is his best Yellow Cords and orange tee shirt,
Ronnie T thought he looked so cool,
But Ronnie B all dressed in black, knew otherwise and said,
You look like a raspberry ripple you fool

At the village hall was a shindig,
And the lads went there for to have some fun,
The yellow cords and orange shirt caused a sensation,
And the two Ronnies to their tent did run.

After dumping the clothes in a litter bin, the drive to Scotland was not too far
They spent their second night by Loch Lomond, and slept inside their car.
The car was overrun by midges, and they didn't get to sleep that night.
So the set of early next morning, when the sun was shining bright.

They drove through beautiful scenery, and saw many lochs passing by,
And that afternoon caught a ferry, to the bonny Isle of Skye.
They pitched their tent by a cottage, and it felt good to be alive.
Until the sound of bagpipes woke them up, just before half past five.

Later they stopped in the Cairngorms,
At a famous German skiing lodge one day,
And Ronnie B ordered two lagers for it was his turn to pay.
Ronnie T went to the toilet and got locked inside the loo,
And as no one there spoke English and he didn't know what to do.

At last a young English lad came in, after forty five minutes had gone,
And he went to fetch the landlord, which embarrassed the other Ron.
He shoulder charged the cubicle, and Ronnie T fell on the floor.
He didn't stop to drink his lager but ran out of the skiing lodge door

Many other things happened on that holiday which cost all of twenty quid
They went straight home the very next day then had a week in Brid
The car battery packed up, the tent collapsed and rain soaked all their gear
What a rotten holiday, but we went back to Brid the following year.

Hope for the coming year

To keep a new year's resolution is always difficult to fulfill,
I'll give up chocolate, biscuits and puddings, I will, I will, I will.
By the second week in January, the whole thing's gone to pot,
I've found where my wife's hidden the goodies, and I've eaten all the lot.

New Year is really no different, than any other time,
But we need a time to start again, and this time of year seems fine.
Looking back on the old year, on television we have seen,
It often seems all doom and gloom, upon the silver screen.

Hope for a better future, is at the forefront of our mind,
All problems of the past, let's leave them far behind.
Each New Year brings us hope, of some new exciting thing.
All sorrows are in the past, what wonders can this New Year bring.

Without hope for a better future, there's nothing to look forward to,
A brighter new year for ourselves, and others, is what I wish for you.
Each New Year we remember, the happy times and sad,
Those we will always remember, and the good times that we had.

A new year is full of promise, of doing the things we would like to do,
Spending more time with friends and family, many things to look forward to.

New books to read, new friends to make,
Pictures to paint and cakes to bake for tea,
New places to visit and new sights to see,
So let's make this New Year become a reality.

Let's have a vision for the year, and look forward to new things,
Let's open up new horizons, and fly on eagle's wings.
Only we can do it, so let's dream dreams of every kind,
And look forward to tomorrow, and discover peace of mind.

Joy and Peace
(A Christmas Poem)

Christmas is a special time for every girl and boy,
With Mince pies and fairy lights and that extra special toy.
But many people in this world live with wars that never cease,
And Christmas is the saddest time bereft of joy and peace.

At Christmas we celebrate a saviour, born in a cattle stall,
He came from heaven's holy realm, to bring peace and joy to all.
Jesus is the answer to all this war and strife,
To bring forgiveness to all mankind, he offered up his life.

Let's pray this Christmas that wars will cease,
As to the Prince of Peace we sing
And people everywhere will raise their hands, at the coming of the King.
He is the only answer to every man, woman, girl and boy,
Let the whole earth fix their eyes on him, the bringer of peace and joy.

Let's lift our eyes up once again, with the shepherds long ago.,
And see heaven's host appear, and marvel at that wondrous glow.
Let is sing our carols this Christmastime, and let our wonder never cease,
And sing praises to the new born king, Jesus the bringer of Joy and peace.

Let the people everywhere pray to him, throughout this coming year.,
That hearts may be changed from hate to love, and bring an end to fear.
Let the Christmas spirit fill the hearts, of those of every race and creed,
Let peace and joy replace all hate, all bitterness and greed.

A Tribute to David Barnes (Barney)

Unlike other characters in my short stories in this book David Barnes was a real person and friend. He was a simple soul and touched the hearts of many people.

Also people like David should be remembered.

This is a tribute to Barney a character who lived above the shops on St. John's Green on Kimberworth Park estate in Rotherham. He died in January 2013 at the young age of 50.

Everyone called him Barney but he once asked me to call him David.

I know nothing of his early life but got to know him quite well over a number of years.

He attended Rotherham College where I worked as a joinery lecturer. Barney enrolled on a NVQ Level 2 bricklaying course. This was a three year course and Barney attended one day per week for seven years and was finally awarded his certificate.

He got a job as a bricklayer with the company building the rent office on St. John's Green and sadly his bricklaying wasn't up to standard.

They gave him the job of mixing mortar for the bricklayers who complained about bits of paper in the mix..

Barney's reply was "I did exactly what you told me to do. Put 40 shovels of sand into the mixer and throw in a bag of cement".

I occasionally taught David, as I always called him, for maths and science etc. A few years ago I was driving away from church after the morning service when out of nowhere, David jumped in front of the car. Thinking that something was wrong I stopped the car and opened the window. David said the last thing that I expected.

"Ron what's the area of a circle"

Pi r^2 "I said.

" How do you find Pi" he said.

"Divide the diameter of the circle into the circumference" I said. Then off he went as happy as Larry.

 David attended church on a regular basis for a number of years and the following Sunday as we were coming out of the service David popped up in the back pew and with a loud voice said "what's the area of a circle again"?

David was a character, not wealthy, with simple tastes, and will be sadly missed by many people on the estate, in Staniforths, at the TARA and at the church. It was rumoured that they had to lay someone off at the betting office on Oaks Lane after he died.

David always wanted to earn his own money and in his own way worked for what he had. So he became a window cleaner.
He was a slightly better window cleaner than he was a bricklayer. I was told the other day that he was fine but only if you had round windows.
He had a mini for a while but he will be remembered carrying extension ladders, triangular ladders and a bucket up and down the estate.

Carol in Staniforths told me an amusing story.

A few years ago one summers afternoon he was cleaning windows at a house where young children were playing in a small paddling pool and David was up his ladder cleaning windows. The mother took her children out for a while and David not wanting to waste the water stripped down to his boxer shorts, sat in the pool and had a bath. When the lady returned he was back up his ladder again, a much cleaner person.

David had a paper round at one time and could be called upon to deliver papers if someone failed to turn up. The previous owner of the shop told me that if he came back soaking wet he would take of his wellingtons and socks and sit with his feet on the heater at the back of the shop

Friday coffee mornings in church are not the same without him.
He would bring his Daily Star crossword in for us to help him finish it. He had a very good general knowledge and it was usually only 2 or three questions he needed help with.
Week after week he would say the same thing.
"Him in betting office is good but you lot are better". Then he would order everything on the menu. Bacon sandwich, pikelets and toasted teacakes and then proceed to give his teacakes away.

I had been to buy a sandwich and bumped into David and said do you have a sandwich for lunch and he said no I have fish and chips. It turned out that he had eaten fish and chips every day for years. This could have contributed to his early death.

Finally there was a side to David that many people didn't realise.

On his window cleaning rounds, and especially around Christmas he would often take gifts to people who were in need a bag of potatoes here a small bag of coal there and if someone gave him a tip he would always buy them something back with the money.

We will miss seeing Barney in his Auto Cumpo jacket and bobble hat around the green and around the estate.
Many people who were special to David and cared for him, kept an eye on him and especially the staff at Staniforth's, who took special care of David and made sure that he had something to eat over many years.
His auto compo Jacket came from a member of staff there and even though he had other coats that was special to him.
When he died his funeral was poorly attended so on the 13th January I led a special memorial service for him in St. John's Church on St. John's Green where he spent so much time.
You meet a character like Barney once in a life time and I for one am glad that I knew him.

The Magic Carpet

Ken the Arab was a fine carpet maker,
The son of a princess and a quality royal baker.
They met one day at a show jumping meet.
When he dropped his hot cross buns at her majesty's feet.
She soon fell in love with his iced cherry buns,
And they married next August and had lovely twin sons.

Son number one was destined to become a king,
And inherit the title of Caliph and wear a royal ring.
The second son Ken missed out on both titles and wealth,
But had all the good looks. and was blessed with good health.
He was apprenticed to a carpet maker, that wasn't so bad
And made fine Persian carpets, in ancient Baghdad.

His twin brother Dick the Caliph, travelled the world of his day
While Ken made fine carpets for minimum pay.
If only I could travel like my brother Dick said he,
When a genie appeared on the carpet maker's knee.
Spread out your finest carpet said the genie to Ken,
And in a moment I'll make you the envy of all men.

He waved his wand in a wizarding way,
And created a magic carpet on that very day.
Sit on the carpet and say two yabba dabba dos,
And it will take you and your friends wherever you choose,.
This was the start of magnificent adventures galore,
As Ken and his carpet, travelled along many a sea shore.

He arrived at all the places ahead of his brother Dick,
Who wondered how Ken arrived at these places so quick.
He kept his secret well, as the genie had suggested,
And never travelled by carpet, until his food was digested.
He carried on making carpets, and made quite a lot.
And sold them to Merlin, in ancient Camelot.

Now unknown to Ken and his lovely wife Marie,
Merlin was none other than Ken's magic genie.
He sold all of Ken's carpets to knights of the round table,
And gave the profits to Ken, whenever he was able.
Ken soon became rich, beyond a man's wildest dreams,
And lived on fish fingers and vanilla ice creams.

Now Ken and Marie had a kingdom of their own,
And Ken's daughter Poppy they placed on the throne.
In a land across the English Channel, far away from Baghdad.
The kingdom they named Yorkshire, a name that's not bad.
And is famous for its cycle races, its pudding and it's tykes,
Who write poems in a strange dialect, and ride around on small bikes.

Ken loved his magic carpet and used it with care,
And gave rides over to Ireland, much cheaper than his rival Ryanair
He took fourteen people to Ireland, three times each day,
 In relative comfort with only ten pounds to pay.
All of this happened in the far distant past
But sadly the carpet's lost forever, for good things never last.

My Ten Pet Hates

(Not in rank order)
Old fashioned courtesy doesn't cost
But it's an art today that's sadly lost

People who cross fields and don't shut gates
Is on the list of my ten pet hates.

When walking in the country or out for a ride
To see rubbish dumped is a thing I can't abide
People who don't indicate is also on my list
And drivers who sound their horn and also shake their fist

Drivers who don't acknowledge
When you let them in the queue
Also belong on in my top ten hate list too
Drivers with no patience and try to get past
And then overtake you and are going far too fast

Those who throw litter is another modern sin
Along with dog owners who don't use the provided doggy bin
People who have no patience with vulnerable elderly folk
And treat them as idiots or some kind of joke

People on trains who put their bags on a seat
Whilst people are standing is something I often meet
These pet hates could be endless but I thing you've got the gist
There are many more things I could put on my personal hate list

My Viking inheritance.
Some of this is true

The Vikings came to England in seven hundred and ninety three,
And Ronald Olaf Townsveld Splat chopped down a chestnut tree.
Now Ron Olaf was a carpenter and a handsome chap at that,
He wore fashionable clothing and a fur lined bearskin hat.
He built two houses in Yorkshire of wood and straw and mud,
Like the one that Shakespeare lived in, and his work was very good.
But he had a problem tenant, who refused to pay the rent,
So he beat his tenant soundly, and so was exiled down to Kent

His ancestors lived there for centuries, before they moved away,
For a farmers work is very hard, and done for little pay.
Grandfather George was a groom, and his father John caught rats,
But his wife Mary Jane Taylor, thought that this was a job for cats.
George became a groom in Chertsey in nineteen hundred and one,

And then moved to Yorkshire and had eight kids including a son called Ron.
Ron had four children, all descendants of Ronald Olaf Townsveld Splat.
His son Ron also was a carpenter, and a handsome chap at that.

<u>The Church Tea Rota</u>

I'm on teas again in the church kitchen what can possible go wrong
Three teas please said Sheila one black, one weak and one strong
A glass of milk said Martha and you've hidden the good biscuits again
The chocolate one's are in that cupboard you're becoming quite a pain.

Three coffees please said Patricia one black, one weak and one strong
I'll make my own said Carol you always get mine wrong
Now Val was serving teas whilst the coffees I started to make
And Peter asked for a decaf how much more of this can a poor man take?

Denise saw the weak tea I was pouring and in a loud voice said "Hey up"
I'm not drinking that weasel, I'll have a teabag in a cup.
Then she and three others invaded kitchen for to make their own drink,
While I was poised like a coiled spring to serve people with coffee,
But trapped by the kitchen sink.

The orders were now coming in thick and fast
I'm sure there's something I've missed
Next time I'm on teas with Derek I'm writing things down on a list
Now it's pot washing time in the kitchen,
With cups, teaspoons, milk jugs and the biscuit plate,
People who leave dregs in the bottom of their cups,
Is something that I certainly hate.

Pots now washed, dried and stored away,
Our duty is done until some other day.
I can now go home for my dinner,
And on computer I can play.
But this is not to be.
For when I look through the serving hatch, I see something is amiss,
There are five empty cups at the bottom table, that need washing,
And the culprits are Janet, Diane, Denise, Pat and Chris.
I'll soon be on teas again in the church kitchen,
But next time I'm coming down hard.
By only serving certain people with refreshments,

And certain other people from this Sunday are barred.

A Transfiguration Hymn
Tune Ode to Joy

On a mountain what a story
See the Lord all shining now
As he prayed to God in heaven
Peter, James and John stood by

Two great prophets what a story
Spoke of Jesus' future then
Filled with fear and awe and wonder
Peter, James and John stood by

See the Lord in shining glory
Tell the world this story now
Shine on us each day Lord Jesus
Shine on us dear Lord today

God spoke to them, what a story
"Listen to the son I love
All that Jesus does has pleased me"
Peter, James and John stood by

Tell your friends of this great story
All that Jesus Christ would do
How he walked to death and glory
Peter, James and John stood by
See the Lord in shining glory
Tell the world this story now
Shine on us each day Lord Jesus
Shine on us dear Lord today

We are part of his great story
If we follow him as Lord
One day we shall see him shine with
Peter, James and John on high

See the Lord in shining glory
Tell the world this story now
Shine on us each day Lord Jesus

Shine on us dear Lord today

The Trauma of Shopping

On certain afternoons, when many do their shopping,
Men go round the Isles, often without stopping.
This usually happens before Christmas once every year,
They buy pork pies and crisps and fill trolleys full of beer.
But women are different, and take their time when shopping each week,
Selecting things carefully and many bargains they seek.

Letting men do the shopping is often a folly,
They put many strange items into the shopping trolley.
So men often sit in cars, reading their daily newspaper.
While wives put up, with this weekly shopping caper.
Says she, just look at those long checkout queues
Says he, there's not much happening in the news

When in supermarkets choosing their food,
Many customers are often rude,
Once in a store at the Christmas checkouts,
Two ladies were fighting over a string bag of sprouts.
It's the last bag and it's mine and I saw it first,
And during the "tug of war" the string bag it burst.

Packing shopping bags is seen as an art,
Because certain items should be kept apart.
A pet hate of my friend Ken's it should be said,
Is when tins of soup, have squashed a loaf of bread.
Bananas can also be ruined at the weekly shop,
When putting a frozen chicken on the top.

Unpacking the car can also be a pain,
On a winter's day in driving rain,.
Celia bought a lasagne for a special occasion,
But the outcome was a startling revelation.
Husband Ken who's always been right,
Instead of keeping it flat carried it upright.

The lasagne's ruined our Celia remarks,
It cost me eight pounds, from Marks and Sparks.
Now Ken's so laid back it's no problem to him,

We'll serve it in the dark and feed it to Richard and Tim.
Just for once in your life, can you get things right?
We can't get another lasagne at this time of night.

Now Ken and an idea like he often had,
He's always been clever since he was a lad.
What is it now, said Celia with a sigh,
We'll cover it with mash, and say its shepherd's pie.
Now Celia was mad and their eyes they did meet,
And what she did next I cannot repeat.

Short of Money in Old Age
(*Short of money for train Spotting*)

I'm a pensioner now and it's not very funny,
I have to be careful with my small amount of money.
When you retire money's hard to come by,
And I'm sorry to tell you I can't even get any PPI.

I find it very difficult to save my meagre cash,
So I thought I'd have to give, my Premium Bonds a bash.
I've had them in for over, thirty years this year,
I've not won a sausage and that is very clear.

I think I'll cash them in and use all the money,
But my wife doesn't think that is very funny.
I've had three good wins of fifty quid she said,
But I've not won enough money to buy a loaf of bread.

If you cash them in now you'll make a mistake,
For the following week could have been your big break.
So I'll have to survive on my pocket money again,
And save up a bit longer for my trip on a train.

I'm a seasoned train spotter I'm proud to say,
And now my visit to London Paddington, is for another day.
Cash from my premium bonds, is now looking quite bleak,
So I'll make do with Doncaster, as I do every week.

My First Car

My first proper car was a Vauxhall Viva I bought it in 1968
It was the same type of car I passed my test in
And everything about it was great.
I parked it in the fairground, knowing Halfords was not too far
When I came back with my chrome cleaner and wax polish
I got straight into the wrong blue car.

I realised my mistake quite quickly and panicked I have to say
And after locking up the wrong motor, found mine several cars away.
I drove straight home to my parents and took them for their first run
Grandma had never been in a car before and was having lots of fun
I polished my car every weekend and cleaned the chrome till it shone
No one had ever had a car in our family so I was the very first one

I went with my family to Whitby and travelled there again and again
To visit my Aunty in Whitby we usually travelled there by train
We travelled through North Yorkshire and fell in love with the moors
It became so familiar that I could have taken people on guided tours.
It took hours to drive there, in the sixties for motorways didn't exist
And driving through York centre is something that I have missed

Now cars were simple in those days but the bodywork started to rot
With two new wings and a front panel and the repair bill was quite a lot
My friend John was a mechanic and a superb craftsman was he.
The cost could have been much higher for he did all my work for free
Despite all the problems with repairs, my blue viva and I travelled far
My car today has perfect bodywork but I really loved my first car.

The Peaky Chappie

My you do look peaky Ken, I'm sure you're not alright,
When you looked in the mirror to shave, I bet you had a fright.
I looked alright this morning, a fine figure of a man,
And I also have an appetite, a good as desperate Dan.

Now Ken was a happy chappie, who made things out of wood,
And listened to his beloved wife, as all good husbands should.

113

But as for looking peaky, he knew that she was wrong,
I'm as healthy as a squirrel, and almost twice as strong.

You're definitely peaky Ken, and it's worried me all day,
I'll send for our daughter who is a nurse, and see what she has to say.
After a thorough examination, her verdict was concise.
You're definitely looking peaky dad, and that's not very nice.

Now Ken needed a second opinion, so he sent for good friend Ron..
Whose knowledge almost equalled Kens, for they both were seldom wrong.
Now Ken and Ron knew almost everything, and he trusted Ron's advice,.
And he knew from past experience, that Ron's verdict would suffice.

Now Ron was working in Ken's shed, and came quickly at Ken's call,
And found Ken looking in the mirror, just inside the hall.
Then to Ron's horror and amazement, Ken's wife said to him.
My you're also looking peaky Ron, and life was suddenly grim.

The men stared at each other, and words in them did fail,
For their reflection in the mirror, made both of them look pale.
Now Ron in a flash of inspiration, which Ken knew he could trust,
Solved the problem immediately, and said, our faces are covered in sawdust.

Wives take heed of this story, for jumping to conclusions is a disgrace,
Before you tell your husband that he looks peaky,
First ask him to wash his face.

Thermal Underwear

I've got to put my Long John's on, for I'm going out today,
To the Worth Valley railway, you know out Keighley way.
For keeping warm in winter, thermals are the best,
Much better than thicker trousers, or rubbing Vick upon your chest.
When I was a lad of twenty, I wore tee shirts and thin shorts,
I never felt the cold back then, and flue I never caught.
I'd go about each winter, and never wore a jacket.
My mother used to tell me off, in fact made such a racket.

But those idyllic days of my youth, are sadly now long gone,
And at my wife's insistence, it's thermals now for poor old Ron.

The Wishing Well

(A short story)

My name is Wellington Bluebottle Dropping and once in every century an ancestor of mine becomes famous.

This is the story of just one of them, the very first Dropping recorded in the secret book of Dropping that has eventually been passed down to me.

It all began seventeen hundred years ago just after the Roman's left England when my great, great etc grandfather Ercol Mammoth Dropping who had just built the first wishing well in a place that one day would be known as Rotherham. He went there to avoid the Saxons when they invaded England during the second half of the fifth century. He accumulated a huge amount of stone after building a local Abbey for the Cistercian monks and carted the stone to where he believed the Saxons would not find him, for they were killing people with funny names. He wisely believed that rather than building a tall building which would be seen for miles he would build a dwelling in the disguise of a well and live in a special room concealed in a side passage in the well itself. All went well, if you'll excuse the 'pun', and after two months and the well was complete. So Ercol who was a stone mason and carpenter by trade furnished his new dwelling with furniture made of seasoned beech and it became known as Ercol's furniture.

He moved in with his wife Tilly (short for Matilda) and their two children Barrow and his sister Gates named after two things that he had invented. They lived in peace for a number of years until Gates brought home her new boyfriend Ding Dong the local magician. Just before they were married by a local priest from Darnall, near the village of Sheffield her dad was not pleased with her marrying a foreigner but thought that having a magician in the family would be useful. Ding Dong Bell to give him his full name turned out to be the perfect son in law. And on his wedding day used a magic spell and turned the dwelling into a wishing well.

Because of his silly name Ding Dong was also hiding from the Saxons living in Masbrough. But Ding Dong Bell had a secret that he told Gates Dropping on their wedding day. Ding Dong was no other than the magician Merlin who a few centuries later would live in Camelot at the court of King Arthur. Gates like all Yorkshire folk couldn't keep water as they say and told her family as soon as the ceremony was over.

Ding Dong inspected their new home which had been extended to include rooms for the newly married couple, and although the well was only a knee's length above the ground it was still visible to the observant Saxon spy. To solve this problem Ding Dong waved his Hawthorn wand and the well became invisible to everyone but himself and other members of the Dropping family. This solved a problem that baffled people for over sixteen hundred years. Why is the road in the ancient village of Kimberworth called **Droppingwell?**
The well remains invisible even to this day and once every ten years descendants of the ancient Dropping clan gather around the well which becomes visible for one hour and drink a toast to Ercol and Tilly Dropping and their family and of course to Merlin the magician, Gates and their daughter Pussy who with her parents still live in the secret rooms in the well and never age.
After the toast they sing the song that has been sung for centuries and children sing it even to this day. "Ding Don Bell, Pussies in the well. Merlin then appears to them and wishes them well. You may wonder what happened to Barrow Dropping the son of Ercol and Tilly. Straight after Gates married Merlin, Barrow married a lovely lass from Derbyshire that strange county full of coal miners and unicorn hunters. He and his new wife Weel Barrow founded a colony at what became Barrow Hill famous for steam engines.
Thus ends the tale of the first of my recorded ancestors.

The Exiled Cricketer

In a jungle far away lived a man called Billy Bray,
Billy was a Yorkshire lad, and exiled there by his old dad,
Billy's dad's heart was almost broken,
For Billy used words that should never be spoken.

Now Billy was an ace at playing cricket,
And had bowled over many a wicket.
His dad was as proud as a man could be,
And imagined his son playing on TV.

But what changed his mind overnight,
And cause father and son to have a fight.
If this was a song it would be a lament,
For Billy signed up to play for Kent.

A crime for a Yorkshire lad back then so the law says
Punishable by exile in the jungle for a year and four days
On his last day in the jungle, his dad and his lawyer came to see Billy,
Come back and play for Yorkshire, they said, and stop being silly.

Playing for Yorkshire at thirty pounds a game will always pay your rent,
Better than the measly fiver they would pay you in Kent.
Now Billy's answer to them drove his dad wild,
I'm staying right here dad, for I'm now the king of the Jungle,
With a lovely wife and a child.

We live here in luxury and money doesn't exist,
And cricket is something, that I've never missed.
His dad was amazed at his answer, and Billy knew he had won,
We're coming here to live with you, they can stuff their cricket my son.

<u>Our Grass is real</u>

As I look out of my window what do I see?
Gardens full of artificial grass and decking,
But not one single tree.
I see this as I look both to the left and to the right,
And I say to myself what a sad sorry sight.

Where do the birds go and the butterflies no one can tell?
Where is the lovely blossom and the Autumn colours as well.
Where are the shrubs and flower that I love to see?
Seeing bare boards with deck chairs is a tragic thing to me.

Where are the fruit and vegetables that used to be grown?
Now that there's nowhere but boxes, for seeds to be sown.
It certainly is a sorry state of affairs,
Does nobody today grow apples and pears?

Then my eyes start to focus on my own piece of land,
And see trees and flowers and don't they look so grand?
There are tomatoes in the greenhouse, lettuces and squash,
We also got some real grass and not plastic for to wash.

We've got squirrels and butterflies and all kinds of birds,
I'm so happy right now that I've run out of words.

Over indulgence

Sally Briggs smoked fifty cigs before she went to bed,
Her best friend Penny said that's too many, or you may end up dead.
Sally said Penny, I don't smoke too many, for a gal of ninety eight,
I smoked twenty after breakfast and I am feeling great.
Another mate called peroxide Kate, also gave her advice,
Stop smoking Sal my long time pal, or it will shorten your life.

Dora Mars ate chocolate bars, about three dozen a day,
Her mother said Dora, I've told you before, put that chocolate away.
Her sister Denise said Dora Please, stop eating Kit Kats tonight,
The reason for this is that her favourite sis, never offered her a bite.

Another best friend Rita, told her to change to Rivita,
For Sally was now twenty stone, as big as an immersion heater
She took her advice, which was very nice, and told her on the phone.
She went on a diet, and kept it very quiet and now weighs eleven stone.

Charlie Greer drank a gallon and half of beer,
Every night of every week,
Every morning without any warning,
His legs came over all weak.

Eighty four pints a week, said dad,
That's putting pressure on your calf,
Cut the amount down by half you silly clown,
So he now drinks only eighty three and a half.

On a Friday nights on the town,
 Charlie is always falling down,
After drinking so much beer.
And his mate Billy Thaw,
Always takes him home in his car
About fifty times every year

<u>My Jumper of Lincoln Green</u>

I have a favourite jumper since I was seventeen,

It is my favourite colour for it is Lincoln green.
I bought it from Waddingtons,
A famous Rotherham Store,
If I had my time over again,
I would have certainly bought two more.

When I wear my jumper I always look so good,
I only wear it now, when,
I'm watching episodes of Robin Hood.
My Jumper size was medium,
And now I'm extra large,
When it needs a piece letting in,
It's my wife who then takes charge.

I've wore it on special occasions,
When I wanted to impress my friends,
They never failed to comment,
Their praise it never ends.
I wore it at my wedding,
With a suit of Lincoln green,
I was the most unusual bridegroom,
That they had ever seen.

I wore it around Holmfirth,
And I was looking fine,
Someone thought I was auditioning,
For Last of the Summer Wine.
My jumper's getting frail now,
And my eyes are often full,

My wife says she'll knit another,
If only she can get some wool.
If she knits me a new one,
My old one I will have to keep,
And wear it in the bedroom,
When I go to sleep.

My Sunday's in the Fifties

Sunday mornings we would play games,
With mates on the green or in the street.
While mum cooked the Sunday dinner,
We kept from under her feet.

It was just after two on Sundays,
Before we got our grub,
Sunday dinner always came,
When dad came back from pub.

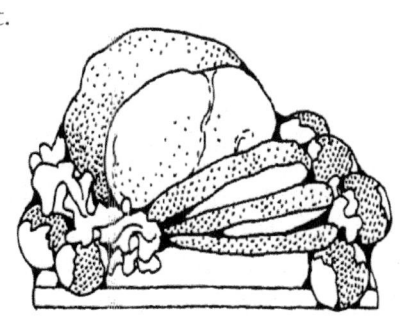

At our house it were always Yorkshire's first,
Complete with mushy peas,
Then roast beef and all the trimmings,
And pop to quench our thirst.

The drink was Northern Dairies orange juice,
From the milkman's cart.
My mother's Sunday dinner,
Were a work of art.

She always cooked some extra food,
For Monday's bubble and squeak.
We called it fry up in our house,
And had some Monday evening,
A highlight of the week.

I can never remember a time,
When mum didn't get it right,
We had simpler meals during the week,
For money then was tight.

For entertainment on Sundays,
Our wireless went on at two.
For Round the Horn, and the Navy Lark,
Just to name but two.

Archie Andrews followed,
That cheeky wooden chap.

Then Sing Something Simple,
Before mum and dad went for a nap.

Wireless in our house is a thing of the past
We have a different Sunday dinner every week
Roast beef dinners are a tradition that wasn't to last.
It's chicken or pasta or a carvery at the pub,
Oh I wish I could travel back,
And eat my mother's grub.

It's now television on a Sunday for me,
With Dr Who on the screen,
I watched Dr Who on a black and white set,
When I was just thirteen.

Kimberwoth Park in the Early Days

There was a pit in Roughwood wood when I was just a kid,
And many men worked there including my neighbour Sid.
The pit closed down in the fifties, and the ruins were full of bats,
On Kimberworth Park in the early days when miners all wore hats.
Kimberworth Park and Wingfield Social Club was built where pit had been,
I worked on it as a joiner there, and remember building a hardwood screen.
Sadly in the second year of this century, the club was burned to the ground,
Arson was suspected, but no culprit could be found.
It was just fields, woods and farm houses, it was a young kid's paradise,
The only shop was called Quibells that sold groceries, milk and kiddies spice.
Spice is a Yorkshire name for sweets, like kali and sweets kept in jars,
There were lucky bags and black jacks and penny arrow bars.
They also sold great big bottles of pop made by Tizer and sarsaparilla too,
And gob stoppers and flying saucers, bubble gum and penny chew.
Quibells was a farmhouse and so was Abdy Farm pulled down in fifty nine,
Replaced by the Domino that hallowed drinker's shrine.
The farmer's wife sold orange juice, which kid's thought was cool,
They drank it in the morning on their way to Redscope school.
The estate was just an enormous playground in nineteen fifty five.
The fields and woods were our domain, it was good to be alive.

<u>Not Cabbage Again Mum</u>

Why do I always have to eat mashed potatoes and cabbage?
I'd rather have egg and chips for my tea

Shut up and eat your dinner lad, or I'll tell thy father on thee.
But I really hate cabbage, and that turnip you mash with potato is vile,
Turnip and cabbage are good for you son, so give it a rest for a while.

Why can't I go out to play mum me mates are waiting for me?
I want you to keep clean son, your auntie's coming to tea?
Why do I have to stay in, she'll give me a big sloppy kiss,
Me mates are making bows and arrows, it's something I can't miss.
Shut up and be quiet lad, I don't want you showing me up,
And be sure to mind your manners lad,
And drink properly from your cup.

Can I go to the pictures dad,
There's a film on at the Odeon that's so funny?
You'll have to wait till payday lad, till you get your pocket money.
It's not fair dad, my friend Phillip always has enough money to spend,
His parent's haven't got four kids and a great dog to feed son,
So stop asking for money now, you'll drive us both round the bend.

Oh no not cabbage again mum?

Wassa Matta Again
(A Short Story)

During my railway days in Wassa Matta Ken and I met the man who was to change our whole lives.

In an old railway workshop lived the man who had invented the image enhancer, a camera that relayed images from the front and back of the locomotive onto a screen in the cab. On steam trains in the twentieth century the driver and fireman had to stick their head out of the side window of the cab to see with great difficulty the front of the engine. This great man had solved this problem. This marvelous invention enabled the trains to travel at 200 miles per hour in complete safety. One afternoon we visited his workshop deep inside the tunnel near the entrance to Shanghai. Our eyes were drawn to a strange octagonal dark glass structure in a corner of his cave. On enquiring on its purpose We were told that it was a prototype time machine as yet untested. The inventor who called Jimmy Tupp was known by the name of Makey Tupp because of the inventions that came from his unique mind. He had a lot in common with Ken because of his vast knowledge of almost every subject. Makey offered to let us travel as his companion on the trial run of the time machine known as the **T,TRIAGO** which stood for **T**ime **T**ravel **I**n **A** **G**lass **O**ctagon. This was abbreviated to **Triago** for simplicity

The next morning on April the first, Makey Tupp Ken and I entered the Triago which to our surprise was bigger on the inside. In the back of our mind we wondered if Jimmy alias Makey Tup was in fact the first time Lord and we were in the prototype of a TARDIS.
We set the time dial to over 3000 years in the past to the very beginning of Wassa Matta on the border of Saudi Arabia and Iraq.

In an instant we appeared in a vast desert and met a tribe of over 2000 nomads led by a man named Ken Wassa and his partner Ronnie Matter.

Each nomad had a ten foot long shovel supplied by the Cairo spade and shovel company and imported from the Chislett iron works in Kimberworth Deer Park.
As the excavation got deeper and deeper, some of the locals joined in the digging using hoes with twenty foot wooden handles and as they marched on to the site every morning you could hear them singing High Hoe, high hoe and off to work we go.
The Arab foreman was called Abbud Weiser who had studied geometry and engineering with the greatest scholars on earth and Abbud would play a crucial part in the years to come and change the world as we know it, inventing steam power 3000 years before James Watt.
At over seventy feet down the diggers struck and outcrop of rock and after thousands of tons of sand had been cleared discovered an opening which was actually a one hundred foot tunnel.

Fortunately the rock was extremely soft and within a month the tunnel was three thousand yards long and over twenty five feet in diameter. Some of the workers remained outside and constructed stone steps to the entrance and by using a timber cage and a series of pulleys invented by Abbud Weiser, formed a means of travelling to and from the surface.

Ken Wassa and his partner Ronnie Matter decided to build a new world beneath the desert and this is how the land of Wassa Matta was born.

As the tunnel progressed every mineral and plant that existed on earth was discovered, catalogued and used to build this new land. Vertical air shafts were constructed along the tunnel which became wider in places as new towns were built for the growing population. It was at the exits of these vertical shafts that new plants were discovered and many of earth's legends of lost tribes or civilisations were based on the people entering Wassa Matta through these shafts and setting up home in Wassa Matta. Ken and I were humbled to meet our distant ancestors and we shed many tears when we left.

Makey Tupp, Ken and I time travelled back one hundred years to see the progress in Wassa Matta.

After one hundred years we saw the railway network built by Abbud Weiser and his apprentices. We were fortunate enough to meet his grandson Much Weiser who took Makey and us on a tour of the first one hundred railway stations. We travelled on the Ronnie Matta Express and to our great surprise the first station we stopped at was named after Makey Tupp

And the next was called Ken Wassa Junction.

On one memorable occasion we went back to the beginning and took Abbud Weiser to the early nineteenth century and introduced him to George Stephenson and Robert Trevithick, and I would like to think that the railway system that we know today was a direct result of that historic meeting between a Geordie a Cornishman and a resident of Wassa Matta. We next took Budda to Belgium in 1876 where he met Brewer Carl Conrad and he named his new beer in honour of this famous Wassmattapian. Today Budweiser is known throughout the world.

At last our 3000 year tour was over and I settled down to write a detailed history of The Strange World of Wassa Matta. Makey Tupp and his time machine disappeared in the early sixties and coincidently Dr Who appeared on our TV screens that same year.

The End

Dodo's and Cleopatra

If I had a time machine, this is what I'd do,
I'd go back to Mauritius, and get two dodo's,
And take them to London Zoo.
I'd do the same with the woolly mammoth,
And other extinct animals the same,
And others that were victims of,
Some greedy hunter's game.

I'd visit ancient Egypt, and get Cleopatra's crown and shoes,
I'd then take pictures of Atlantis, and feature them on the news.
I'd bring back for a visit famous people, who now are long dead,
As seen on the cinema, by the famous Bill and Ted.
I'd bring back the Great Pyramid's architect,
To explain to us how they were made,
I'd visit Camelot's blacksmith and see how to make a sword blade.

If I had a time machine, I'd go some special place and stop.
I'd visit Thomas Chippendale and work in his wood shop.
On these special visits, I'd not do things by halves,
I'd visit Grinling Gibbons, and watch him as he carves.
I'd visit Leonardo, and watch him paint the Mona Lisa,
In sixteen century Florence, and wouldn't need a visa.
I really will do none of this, as sad as it may seem.
For I am in my bed right now, and have just woken from a dream.

I Am An Avid Reader

I am the reading group, which meets on Thursday night,
We read a different book each month, one that seems just right.
We've read an eclectic mixture, and dozens we have had,
Some books were amazing, but many books were quite bad.

The librarian is called Wendy, a lovely lass is she,
And nothing is too much trouble, she often has helped me.

I am an avid reader, and have many books at home,
On every subject you can name, from poetry to ancient Rome.

Sometimes I have to lose a book, for another to take its place,
Sadly this must happen, for I'm running out of bookshelf space.
We've bookshelves in each bedroom, in my office and in garage too.
In every room, within our house, except the upstairs loo.

Now with almost two thousand books, it's becoming quite a pain,
I've often been on Amazon, and bought the same book once again.
I have books of all sizes and colours some are red and some are grey,
I started cataloguing all my books, but gave up this I'm sad to say,
I've lost track where I'm up to, it will take me thirty year.
I was seventy one last August; I won't finish the job I fear

When heaven revealed its glory

When the King of Kings was born,
Angels and archangels came as never before,
It took this one momentous occasion,
To open heaven's door.

Such an honour unprecedented,
Rejoiced in a new born child,
Lowly shepherds were astonished,
As the host of heaven went wild.

Why not appear before kings and priests,
For an honour on them bestow?
The shepherds may have wondered,
But God's wisdom they could never know.

God favours those the world looks down on,
And the shepherds were the lowest of the low.
The angels bade the shepherds to go to Jesus,
And worship him in his stall,
Not realising the honour they'd been given,

To be the first to worship Jesus, who is the Lord of all.

But do we really know what happened,
On that special night so long ago?
And how momentous was that occasion,
To bring heaven's host down below.

The shepherd were awe struck,
And it must have changed their lives somehow,
But does that have the same impact
On people who are alive now?

Many today see Christmas as a celebration,
A party time with food, drink and other special things.
But do they see what the shepherds saw,
A myriad of light and heavenly wings?

When the angels came down from heaven,
Glad tiding for to bring.
To announce that this vulnerable new born child,
Was Almighty God himself, our King.

The Yorkshire Lass at Derby Uni

(The next three poems are about three lovely sisters, the eldest being the first poem)
I wrote a poem about one and the other two wanted a poem too)

Stephen has three daughters,
All bonny bright and keen,
But the one who stands out from the rest,
Is Charlotte Emmeline.
Now Charlotte is at Derby uni, and things are going fine,
She spends her evenings with her friends,
Eating chips and drinking wine.

She's going to be great one day,
Organising nationwide events,
And selling tickets at the gate, and putting up the tents.
Now Charlotte had ambitions to be a singer once,

And making her family proud and glad,
But Charlotte's singing dreams faded fast,
After singing lessons from her dad.

But music was still in her blood, but where should she begin.
So she packed in her singing lessons, and bought a violin.
For four long years she practised hard, but all this also was in vain,
The neighbours though it sounded like, one hundred cats in pain.
Now Derek and Ron her advisors, will help her on her way,
And make sure this bonny lass will not give up,
And make us proud of her one day.

They'll give this Yorkshire lass elocution lessons,
And teach her how to really sing and dance,
They've trained many a famous person, in England and in France.
They once taught a Newcastle lad, to sing 'On Iltley Moor Baht Tat'.
To train a Gordie to have a Yorkshire accent, doesn't get better than that.
And with their help our Charlotte, will soon achieve her ambitions,
Derek and Ron will train her well with the usual conditions.
Yes she will, and soon she will be seen,
Organising national festivals,
That's our tall and charming, often alarming Charlotte Emmeline.

A delegate in the making

Sister No 2
Close to the church on St. John's Green,
Lives a bonny lass called Martha Jean,
She has so many talents for all to see,
But her greatest skill is in making tea.

Her ambitions though are way up high,
To work for the United Nations by and by,
But first to Hull Uni, to get a one, one,
As predicted by her mentors,
The famous Derek and Ron.

A UN delegate she wants to be,
This lass who's exceptional at making cups of tea,
But she's got to put this amazing skill behind her,
As Derek and Ron so often remind her.

She'll make us proud one day she will,
And her UN dreams she will fulfill,
She'll move so fast no one will catch her,
That modern day Maggie Thatcher.

But no she'll be much better by far,
And drive to the UN in a Rolls Royce car,
No simple delegate for our Martha Jean,
She'll be the greatest secretary general
The UN has ever seen.

This is the path our Martha's now on,
All due to the training by Derek and Ron,
She can be anything that she wants to be,
And also make a stunning cup of tea.

Derek and Ron those most modest of men,
Could see her potential from the age of ten,
They've supported her for many years,
And to Martha Jean they send three cheers.

At last she's just seventeen,
That lovely lass called Martha Jean,
She having driving lessons from now on,
So we'll keep off the roads says Derek and Ron.

The Little Sister

You've heard of Charlotte Emmeline,
And her lovely sister Martha Jean,
The industrious pair from near St. John's Green,
But these two young ladies to be fair to them,
Are sober and upright citizens from Sunny Rotherham.

I heard this sad tale from Charlotte,
And I really must believe her,
About her younger sister ,
The one and only notorious Eva.
Eva Hamilton is her name,

And party popping is her game.

This teenage party animal can often be seen,
In the church kitchen, singing Dancing Queen.
She's pretty and clever and ever so kind,
But her social life, leaves her sisters far behind,
When asked by Derek to join the local quiz,
She said she'd rather be at a party and drink Bucks Fizz.

So Derek and Ron those most humble and sober of men
Asked her politely once again
But our Eva who is once again hale and hearty
Said sorry chaps I'm going to yet another party

The lads went away shocked and feeling rather sad,
And had a word with her mum and dad.
But her parents laughed at them, and didn't even dither,
The said hard luck boys, we're going to the party with her.

So the lads reported her to the church PCC,
But the consensus of that group was to let her be,
And if you ever see the sisters together, you'll certainly get a shock,
Charlotte and Martha will both wear slacks,
And Eva Hamilton a party frock.

Why Do Pigeons Nod Their Heads?

There are strange things that happen,
And no answer can be found,
Like why do pigeons nod their heads,
When walking on the ground?
Why do some tea pots dribble when filling up your cup.
And when you drop your bread and butter on the floor.
Why does it always, land the wrong side up?

Why do I nod off in my chair,
When watching my favourite show?

And when I smuggle in a chocolate bar,
How does my wife always know?
And when I nod off in my chair when holding a cup of tea
Why is the cup always full and wets my trouser knee?

Why do animal lovers always look like their own dogs?
And why do tadpoles in my pond always turn into frogs?
Why do the nicest Bramley apples on my tree,
Always fall upon the ground.
When to buy them in the shops today,
You pay one pound fifty pence a pound.

Why are traffic lights when I am out, always showing red?
When I am in a hurry, or want to get home to bed.
Some say the answer is something to do,
With something called 'sod's law'
Others say it's because I was born under some unlucky star.
But there's a simple answer, and I think I'll have a go,
There are answers to some questions, that I will never know.

My Bright Blue Spoon

I have a favourite spoon; I've had it over forty years,
It's been with me through thick and thin,
Through laughter and through tears.
I bought it from Morrisons, in nineteen eighty three,
I use it at my breakfast, and for my pudding after tea.

It's no longer manufactured; it's one of a kind,
I tried to buy a knife and fork to match, but these I cannot find.
It has a bright blue handle and I'll use it all my life,
All this may quite strange to you, as it does to my wife.

I take it with me on holiday, it's with me as I go,
I eat my cereal very early, so my wife doesn't know.
For forty years I also have had a favourite dish
Which I use for cereal puddings and fish

Things never taste the same,
If I use another dish and spoon,
I'm now expecting two men in white coats,
 to come and get me very soon.

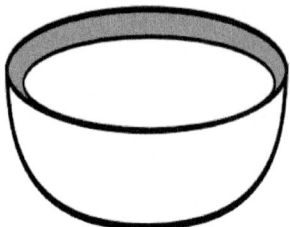

The Parallel Rons
Another Short Story

You may have heard of parallel worlds, where there is another you living in another Rotherham in another Earth. I discovered that another me had followed a different path. Well by some weird quirk of fate I can now see and experience my parallel life. I discovered this when watching Mastermind and for some unknown reason I answered all the questions on nuclear physics and understood the subject as well.

This disturbed me and my family who thought that I being a professional litter picker, that I was of low intelligence. This is when my life changed forever. I was picking litter in a back street in Rotherham when I came upon a strange blue box about five centimetres square with a green button on one side. So like an idiot I pressed the button and suddenly appeared in this parallel world and to my amazement stood facing a young man who was the exact likeness of me. He was so good looking it was uncanny. Straight away he remarked "so it worked at last"!
He went on to explain that he had invented a temporal replacement actuality machine, a small box with a green button, and TRAM for short. He designed this machine so that could trace DNA across parallel worlds and bring the closest match back to his world. I was gobsmacked as he explained that by this process some of his knowledge could be transferred to his parallel twins and vice versa.

Hence my sudden knowledge of Nuclear Physics and I learned that there was no litter within two miles of his house. By using TRAM I went back home and told my parents that I was going on a month's holiday with a friend and not to worry. Back on Earth mark 2, the other Ron and I became the best of friends. He told his family that he had met me by accident and that I was possibly some distant relative. We were both in our early twenties and single. I spent some time in the university for young geniuses where he worked and with my new knowledge helped him with his work. Litter picking would never be the same again. Together we improved his TRAM and turned it into a time machine and travelled together to many parallel Earths and formed a team or seventeen Rons who together pushed the boundaries of science to new limits.

We developed a way of producing a limitless amount of fresh water from the atmosphere, similar to rain but on demand. We then produced a form of energy using surplus water. This revolutionary fuel could replace petrol, heat our homes, cook our food and give unlimited power to our factories at very little cost. This angered the power companies who moved into the field of hydroponics with the surplus water now available to them.

Each of the seventeen Rons we genius's and when they eventually returned to their respective worlds, became celebrities overnight. Each Ron had a TRAM box and visited the first nuclear scientist once a year and had the most unusual birthday parties ever.

This year is the fiftieth anniversary of the first TRAM stop and I am pleased to say that we are all alive and healthy partly due to the healthy breakfast cereal we developed from waste plastics and recycled cardboard thirty years ago. It tastes horrible but it's good for you.
I am still a litter picker by trade but now a very clever one.

The Sea

A life on the ocean wave
Now that's the life for me.
On a sailing ship in the tropics
Upon the deep blue sea.

A tireless sailor I would be,

And work all day and night.
I'd dance a merry horn pipe,
Which is not a pretty sight.

As captain of a galleon,
I'd work even harder,
I'd fire our mighty cannon,
And sort out that Armada.

I'd chase them round to Blackpool,
And give them all a shock,
For when I ran out of ammo,
I'd fire sticks of Blackpool rock.

As captain of a merchant ship,
I'd sail to brand new lands.
And feed on tropical fruit trees,
And lie on golden sands.

The sea is a wondrous place,
But only when it's calm,
I'd want to be on dry land,
In every tropical storm.

I'd love to be a sailor,
Upon the tropical seas,
Feeling the deck beneath my feet,
And the sun upon my knees.

I'd live on mangoes and coconuts,
And produce of the sea,
A life on the ocean wave,
Now that's the life for me.

The Butcher's Shop on St. John's Green

There's been a butcher's shop on St. John's Green,
For sixty years or more,

The first one was the Coop butchers,
With the fruit shop just next door.

But the butchers now on St. John's Green,
Is used by many people daily,
The secret of its huge success,
Is that it's run by Matthew and by Hayley.

Its meat packs are a bargain,
And its pork pies are just great,
And it's well known for its Christmas club,
Throughout the whole estate.

But recently at weekends,
Something different has happened to that shop,
It is a new sensation,
And caused many young men there to stop.

Meat sales have now gone through the roof,
And steak slices are always running out,
What could have caused this rise in sales?
What is it all about?
The other shop keepers on the green,
Thought their new success unfair,

For how could they compete with a butcher's shop
And two lovely ladies, with multi coloured hair?

Now Hayley and Julia have begun a trend.
Whilst selling cuts of meat,

Ronald Town

The women in Staniforths, have died their hair blue
But honestly, they really can't compete.

So if you want some pork chops,
Or even a piece of boiled ham,
Buy your meat towards the weekend,
And you'll see two young ladies there,
Who are the talk of Rotherham.

The Squirrel That Ate My Sausage
And Others

Nonsense and serious poems and silly short stories
By a Yorkshire man with a weird sense of humour

The Squirrel That Ate My Sausage And Others

Nonsense and serious poems and silly short stories
By a Yorkshire man with a weird sense of humour

Ronald Town

Contents

The Tai Chi Group of St. John's Church
The Famous Yorkshire Highland Games
Around the World by Tandem
The Bag Lady from Kimberworth Park
A Vicious Circle
St. John's mines
I Love My Notebooks
Friends and Neighbours
The Passage to Camelot
Little Boxes
The post Wassa Matta Years
Jesus Calms a Storm
An Abundance of Willies
Reggie Bradshaw's Bread and Jam
The Annual Harvest Supper
My Red Dressing Gown
The Storm
A New Digi Box for Ken
The Summer Fayre
Dingle Witney Troop from Wassa Matta
The Cromford Painters in May
A kitchen of Forest Green
Why are My Legs so Beautiful?
The Perils of Sky Diving
Father's Day and twelve pair of underpants
The Test Run
Barry's Musical Interlude
Thunder and lightning, wind and Snow
Edith
The Quiet Walking Group
My Working Life
Twelve Sheds From My Window
Ties and Jumpers
Shunned By All

Edna's Mini Sub

I'm going to buy a submarine said Billy Bladen's mum
But Billy and his dad were gobsmacked and croaked an E by Gum
I'm going to the navy surplus shop and see about a sub
Her husband Horace said to Billy lets go down to the pub

In the Crown and Pig, Horace with pint in his hand, he said to his son Billy
Your mother's always been excitable but she's never been this silly
A submarine is ridiculous dad; in fact I find it quite funny
It'll never happen in a month of Sundays, for Edna's got no money.

Mum's got a big secret dad said Billy with a grin
She had a go on lottery last April and ten million pounds did win
Now Horace was in a state of shock and knocked back a double rum
And all he could think to say to Billy was another E by Gum

Now Edna arrived at the surplus store in eager expectation
And chose a mini sub from the catalogue in a state of jubilation
Edna could already work a sub and knew how to manoeuvre it
She had done a navy training course and had a certificate to prove it

The sub had had its MOT and was in outstanding nick
And the body was of special metal and a good half inch thick
It was painted just how Edna wanted it much to her delight
The colour was a shade of grey and the inside blue and white

Now dad and son left the pub, and to the docks they went
To meet up with Edna and her sub and see how much she had spent
She beckoned them into her sub and announced to both her men
We're sailing off to the Isle of Wight and we'll be there by half past ten

Now Edna had eight million left and said to Billy her lad
I've bought a Ferrari for you son, and an Aston Martin for your dad
They lived a dream life from that day and she bought her husband a pub
And once a month they travelled around the world in Edna's mini sub.

A Squirrel Ate My Sausage

A painting holiday in Cromford is the highlight of my year
Painting with new found friends and the occasional glass of beer
It's the first July to this delightful venue that I've ever been
And I painted a picturesque church and a river scene

Soup and sandwiches we had for lunch
And chatted for an hour with that merry bunch
It's time to mix some paint said Gwen for the trees and for the grass
An exciting time was had by all in that July watercolour class

At breakfast on Wednesday morn we sat at the table
And through the open window
We enjoyed the breeze while we were able
The breakfast came as I chatted to Jane and also to Gwen
When a squirrel came through the window
And ate my lovely sausage just then

A squirrel ate my sausage I just can't believe it
My breakfast was ruined so I just had to leave it
Then back to the art room and I chose an owl to paint
On that Wednesday morn in that venue that was so quaint

I'd finished by lunch and my owl it was complete
And back to the house again for something more to eat
Close that window now I told the waiter whose name was Cyril
I'm not risking my lunch to another blooming squirrel

Choose an animal to draw said Gwen at almost two O'clock
And the animal that I chose that day gave her quite a shock
I started drawing with a pen an animal usually found in the south
Of course it was a red squirrel with a sausage in its mouth

The Great Wall of Shiner

There's a man down our street who's just built a wall
And believe it or not it's nearly fourteen feet tall
I'll tell you something now that is sure to make you laugh
For behind this great wall he keeps an elephant and giraffe
The name of this man is Frederick John Shiner
Of keeping wild animals in his garden he thinks there is nothing finer

From my upstairs window I can see into his zoo
I've just seen an elephant and a rhinoceros too
None of his neighbours now live there by choice
At six every morning the lions make a great roaring noise
Near the motorway fence he dug a great lake yesterday
And the crocodiles that live there keep the burglars away

The neighbours who live adjacent to his plot
Have now moved away and Fred's bought up the lot
The neighbours across the road think what a to do
For a van's just arrived with a camel and kangaroo
He's been reported to the environmental health
But they've put the complaint in a Manila folder
In the basement behind a book on a shelf

Neighbour the lovely Mavis found a polar bear sitting in her garden
Surprisingly the bear said to her. "I do beg your pardon".
Now Mavis thought she was dreaming and sent for husband Mick
Who chased the bear across the road waving a great big stick
Mavis said to Michael that stick has come in handy
I'll just go and sit inside the house and have a double brandy

The whole street is up in arms and have signed a petition
After reading in the Advertiser of a Kimberworth safari expedition
He's made the national papers has Frederick John Shiner
And headlines in the Daily Mirror say the Great Wall of Shiner
The problem is now solved, and our street now has the last laugh
For he's sold all his animals to the Marquis of Bath

So if you have a large garden and are considering having pets
Seek advice first and pay a visit to your local vets
Get a small cat or a rabbit and even two small dogs
And if you build a pond in the garden, then stick to goldfish and frogs
Or even just get a cuddly toy for nothing can be finer
But please, please learn a lesson from Frederick John Shiner

Walk Leader Training
This is a true story

We trained as walk leaders many years ago
And after an hour of theory we had chosen where to go
Look out for risks and dangers and choose the safest route you can
For risk assessment is always part of your walking leaders plan
So we planned a walk together, Val, Colin, Chris and me
And when walking through Barker's Park a man fell from a tree
The man was only stunned, but we walkers four were anxious
He'd tried to recover his dog's lead and fell out of the tree branches

We moved into Bray Plantation a wood just off Oak's Lane
The path we had to follow was most obvious and plain
In this wood were mounds of earth with a hollowed out inside
And Chris and Ron as kids,
Around this wall of death their bikes did ride
So they both climbed this slippery mound,
To re-live this childhood dream
When Chris came back down on his backside,
Letting out an awful scream

So much for health and safety said Colin and Val together
Climbing up wet grassy banks is foolish in this weather
Through the woods we trundled but now in safety mode
And about ten minutes later came out on Wortley Road
We kept to the footpaths and were careful as we crossed Oaks Lane
The dangers were now over and we'll soon be back again
Down that narrow side road, we had not travelled far
When Colin dragged Val from the path, of a great big motor car

The groups came back to church hall to report what risks they'd seen
After going in three directions when leaving St. John's Green
The other groups reported that their walks were all incident free
Then all faces turned around to face Val, Colin, Chris and me
Now we each spoke in turn, in clear and perfect diction
But others in that room thought our walk was a work of fiction
So the moral of this story is when sent to do walk leader training
Wait until everyone else has left; go back inside,
Have a coffee, and pretend that it is raining.

Debbie the Hairdresser

Debbie is a hairdresser and her fame is known far and wide
For cutting the hair of a duchess and many a blushing bride
She cuts hair in Thorpe Hesley in Kimberworth and Scholes
She cuts brown hair, white and ginger and some as black as coals

She often dies hair with wood stain just to save a pretty penny
She once bleached hair with Domestos on a pretty girl called Jenny
She comes to our house often to do the family's hair
She does it in our kitchen and sits us on a chair

She cuts my hair with clippers set at number four
Now the little hair that I once had is on our kitchen floor.
Now during her last visit a strange thing had occurred
It was something quite amazing and utterly absurd

Most of the hair was not from my head where it should have been
It's from the longest eyebrows that Debbie had ever seen
They're so very long says Debbie, and I know that she is right
If they started flapping up and down,
I'd be the first Yorkshire man in flight

Now when she cuts my hair and no one does it finer
The hair from my eyebrows alone will half fill a black bin liner
Now Debbie is a hairdresser whose skill is beyond compare
So get in touch with her today and let her cut your hair

Buffalo Ron

I'd like to go to America and visit the old Wild West
And be Tombstone's carpenter and wear a bearskin vest
I'd make furniture for cowboys and be friends with Wyatt Earp
I'd dress like the Lone Ranger and look a proper little twerp

I'd visit the local saloon each night and drink some ginger beer
And be the bravest cowboy in that town and nothing I would fear
I'd ride a great big white horse of fifteen hands or more
And keep it behind the carpenter's shop with sawdust on the floor

I'd make my living making chairs for the Last Chance saloon
To replace the one's smashed up each night by mad Dan Calhoon
Chair orders would keep on coming and business would be good
And with all the broken bits of chairs, I'll sell as bags of firewood

I'd also start a new Wild West show, and I would from that day on
Shoot a gun from my horse's back, and be known as Buffalo Ron
I'd sell my carpenters shop in Tombstone, and never go back again
And tour the world with my show, from Timbuktu to Spain

I'd move from Spain to Switzerland to Belgium then to France
I'd stay there for quite a while and teach my horses how to dance
But after twenty years or so I'd have a yearning for Yorkshire Pud
And go back to sunny Rotherham and then stay there for good.

Who Invented Fire and the Wheel

(Further adventures of time travelers Ron and Ken)

Many years ago after the Neanderthals became extinct; a family of early humans lived in a cave system in what would thirty thousand years later be known as South Yorkshire. This was a very special family because unknown to us today, they were the very family that developed many things that we now take for granted. We often ask questions like who invented the wheel or made the first pot or who invented clothes and who was the first to produce metal etc? Or who first said E by gum or I'll seethe.

I can tell you the answer to all of these questions because after visiting Wassa Matta, Ken Wassa and I went back in time and as luck would have it landed in the very cave of that gifted family that I have just mentioned.

As we stepped out of our time machine, we were confronted with wonders beyond our wildest dreams. These were early cave dwellers with a full length mirror on the wall and shower cubicle in the corner and sitting at a polished wooden table were four people eating a meal of roast beef and Yorkshire pudding on ceramic plates superbly decorated with flowers and animals. Against one wall of the cave was an open fireplace with a roaring fire made from coal and logs and the smoke was removed by means of a salt glazed flue pipe going through the roof of the cave. We took pictures with our mobile phones, which amazed this Neolithic family.

The family was as surprised as we were and stood up in amazement and stared at our time sphere. They spoke a type of English dialect which we Yorkshire folk understood perfectly easily.
The father was called Erik the Nog and the mother Doone Nog.
The Nog children were Stig Nog and his sister Weenie Nog.
Mum and dad Nog were normal parents, apart from
inventing an alcoholic drink called Egg nog, but their
twin children were born with amazing abilities,
way beyond genius level.
At five years of age they discovered how to make fire
whilst playing marbles with two pieces of flint and
revolutionised the lives of their family and

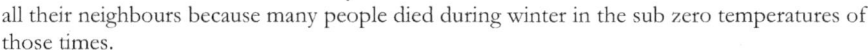

all their neighbours because many people died during winter in the sub zero temperatures of those times.
At eight years of age they invented glass after melting white sand in one of their clay pots and by experimentation invented the mirror.
Whilst planting, what is possibly the first garden in history, with a kind of early wheat, they discovered a mineral ore containing copper; iron ore and galena the ore used to make lead.

With the lead they made pipes which were used to carry water from an overhead stream to storage vessels in all the caves and to showers. They kept a fire burning under a large central copper tank full of water on a flat topped hill and supplied constant hot water for the showers and other uses.
They smelted ores and made metal that could be honed to a superfine edge.
They made tools of every kind and kick started numerous crafts, some of whom are lost to us today.

No weapons were made, for war did not exist.

Each village specialised and trade between neighbouring villages was thriving.
They took us out of the cave system and we were overwhelmed by the sight of ornately decorated carts pulled by pairs of oxen on a track, similar to a railway track, which we were told went for one hundred miles and linked with villages all the way to the great sea.

There were carpenters and blacksmith's shops; bakeries and breweries. Stig and Weenie who were twenty years of age had taught the people various crafts and skills which would be lost for the next twenty five thousand years. Was there anything that Stig and Weenie could not do?
We stayed there for many months and recorded many things which Ken and I used as the basis of our bestselling book *"The Amazing Cave adventures of Stig and Weenie"*. It was sold as fiction but we knew better.

We took the twins back in our time machine to many places throughout history and eventually landed home in the twenty first century.
They loved television and especially Doctor Who and the Flintstones.
They took samples back home with them to study and maybe improve.
Ken and I with our vast knowledge and skill taught them many things.
The world never knew that thousands of years ago South Yorkshire was the cultural capital of the known world.

They met two people in Kimberworth Park and married them, and the Yorkshire dialect was spoken twenty thousand years ago in a cave where the Chislett Centre now stands.
Their partners became Tina Nog and Danny Nog who introduced writing to the twins and somewhere beneath the Chislett Centre on Kimberworth Park in an underground cave, written records of that civilization are buried. Eric and Brenda's son Egg Nog, name in memory of his grandmothr's famous drink, buried these records in a time capsule which may be recovered one day and the revelations contained therein will change the history books for ever.

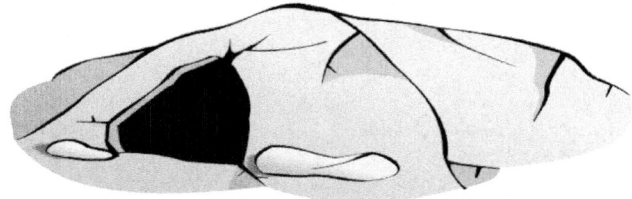

The Multi Talented Kimberworth Lad

Colin was taking pictures at the age of four
Using a mini tripod two feet from the floor
He used a box brownie belonging to his dad
His mother said our Colin is a strange sort of lad

At school had a smaller camera and took pictures of his mates
And sold them for a shilling outside the old school gates
This soon became Colin's regular pitch
And by the age of eight Colin was very rich

His obsession with the camera gave his family many laughs
But by the age of four our Colin discovered maths
He'd learned his times table by the age of five
And with his love of numbers and photos Colin began to thrive

He became so popular and was never on his own
Until he began to practice, on his Boosey and Hawkes trombone
He played it at six every morning
And the neighbours thought he was cool
But you could hear them all cheering as he went off to school

But Colin had the last laugh with all these skills at his command
For he excelled in music and joined his first brass band
He studied music, maths and photography and became quite adept
And his mum was astonished and wondered if he ever slept

He became a teacher in the North West and excelled for many a year
And retired at the age of fifty and took up photography as a career
He joined a local walking group and what a carry on
For there he met a lovely lady by the name of Marion

But the day finally came when he sold his old trombone
And with the cash bought a jacket and a mobile phone
He sold his beloved instrument
For he kept poking Marion in with the slide
And she had a bruised right ear lobe and a pain in her left side

He now sticks to taking photographs with his Nikon D4
And sells them to the walking group who put money
Into his flat cap upon the floor

Price Rises

I can't believe how much it costs today, to buy a loaf of bread,
It used to cost just one and six now it costs one pound instead.
It costs me forty pound or more to fill my tank with fuel today
When I passed my test in sixty five less than two pounds I had to pay

Five hundred pounds in nineteen fifty is sixteen thousand pounds today
I started work in sixty two on less than twelve shillings a day
But it went much further then, it paid my board,
And bought me tools and other stuff
Now twenty pounds a day would hardly be enough

A joiners plane cost two pounds ten shillings in all the sixties decade
Today it costs twenty pounds just to buy the blade
I bought a different tool for work each week in that distant past
I wish I could buy things in shops back then when things were made to last

In seventy four our groceries were only five pounds every week
Now the bill is more than tenfold and our finances are looking bleak
Today's prices would shock my granny if she were here today
When she were a lass she only earned about one shilling a day

I had a shilling pocket money when I were but a lad I'm sure
Kids today have pounds to go to school and then come home for more
It cost sixpence each to go to the pictures when I was only ten
Today its many pounds for each of us in fact it's over ten

Why are prices so high today I do not know the reason?
Two hundred years ago the chancellor would have been hanged for treason
As much as we complain today there's not much we can do
But to cut our cloth and be careful as our mothers used to do

The Coffee Morning Beauties

At our Friday church coffee morning
We start serving round about ten
But one of our main problems is
We have a shortage of men

Women of all sorts come to join us
And buy clothes from size twenty down to ten
But our table is packed with trousers and shirts
That would suit a variety of men

But last Friday something wonderful occurred
As men suddenly began to appear
How was this wonder of wonders possible?
It's not happened for many a year

Was it Ron's dynamic persuasion?
That made these new men appear?
Then in a flash of inspiration
The solution became perfectly clear

The answer lies in the church kitchen
And I'll tell you about it right here
It's fair Maggie and Karen in the kitchen
That has caused these new men to appear

Of course it's their magnetic youthful beauty
That has attracted this new crowd of blokes
And since we realized the answer to our problem
They have been the brunt of all our jokes

So if you're in need of a shirt and some trousers
And you want to get away in a hurry
Don't go to the serving hatch in the church hall
Or the sight of these two raving beauties
Will send your hearts all in a flurry

I Love Trees

(A rant by an ex woodworker)

As a woodworker I have always been fascinated by trees.
I have worked with many timbers during my days in a joiners shop,
in industry and as a joinery lecturer.
I can recognise some types of wood by both appearance and smell when being sawn or machined.
I have made many things with English hardwoods such as oak,
ash and beech.
I can recognise a number of trees, usually by their leaves and fruit.
There is a road called Oaks Lane near where I live and in the fifties when I moved into the area there were a number of oak trees which gave the road it's name.
The majority of these were removed for road building and the building of the then new council estate in the early nineteen fifties when I was about six or seven years of age.
However one majestic oak tree remains on Oaks Lane alongside what was originally the Fire Station.
This magnificent tree is probably hundreds of years old and was there when it was part of the Wentworth Estate.
In even earlier times it was part of the Kimberworth Deer Park.
Trees are the oldest living things on the planet and also the tallest and heaviest things.
The Bristlecone pines in the White Mountains in California
are between 4000 and 7000 years of Age.
In 1964, Donald Rusk Currey a research student killed possibly the oldest tree called Prometheus which was 4900 years old. To this day, there has still never been an older tree discovered. Prometheus was a Great Basin bristlecone pine, and Currey didn't mean to kill it.
It was an accident, and one he didn't really understand the ramifications of until he started counting tree rings.
Basically, Currey got his tree corer stuck in the tree. So stuck that it wouldn't come out. An unwitting park ranger helped him by cutting the tree down, to remove the instrument, and later Currey began to count the rings. Eventually, he realized that the tree he had just felled was almost 5,000 years old – the oldest tree then recorded.
Another tree has since been found but its
location has been kept a secret and the trees
in that area are now protected.

The most impressive trees for me are the California Giant Redwoods.
The Sequoia (Sequoiadendron giganteum) can weigh as much as 6000 tons.
The heaviest is the General Sherman.
And the tallest tree is (Sequoia sempervirens) or coast redwoods which are over 300 feet high and one was discovered in 2008 at 397.7 feet tall. It's name is Hyperion.

I believe one of the saddest things in the natural world today is the destruction of the rain forests.
It is not just the tree producing oxygen disappearing but the plants that grow in the rain forests around the trees that are also destroyed.
 Plants as yet undiscovered that could one day provide food or medicine.
I now do a bit of watercolour painting and have started looking at trees in a new way.
I now see shapes in trees and wonderful colours of leaves in all of the seasons and even the stark beauty of trees when the leaves have fallen.
Next time you are out for a walk of a drive in the countryside, look at the trees and see the wonder of creation.

Trees

Of all the plants on this green earth
The tree is the one of noble birth
It stands so tall in woods and fields
I marvel at the fruit it yields

A thing of beauty and grace that I long to see
Is the mighty splendour of the redwood tree
At three hundred and eighty feet in height
The Coast Redwood is a wondrous sight

This tallest living tree grows above them all
On California's coast it stands so tall
This tree is in the hall of fame
And Hyperion is its name
A dream of mine that may never be
Is to is to walk around the giant redwood tree
To see this tree would be so much fun
Weighing in at over two thousand one hundred ton

General Sherman is its name today
Thirty six feet in width and here to stay
At two and half thousand years or more
And eighty three metres above the floor

It has always been an ambition of mine
To visit the sacred Bristlecone pine
What a privilege it would be to behold
The tree which is over five thousand years old

Old and gnarled Methuselah stands
The oldest tree in all the lands
Before the pyramids it was already old
An amazing sight to behold

To see any of the above would be such a joy
But there are trees I've known since I was a boy
Trees as special that also deserve our praise
Trees that are around us all of our days

There are trees I've climbed in woods and park
All day long till it was almost dark
They are still there for all to see
In woods, gardens, fields and all for free.

The mighty oak, beech and chestnut too
The ash and birch just to name a few
Still bring joy and pleasure to me
For natures greatest wonder is the tree

Getting Lost on a trip to Nottingham

First thing in the morning we're going for a run
We'll set of at six O'clock and have a full day of fun
At the Robin Hood experience and the treat is on me
We'll go to Weatherspoons for lunch and then we will see
A show at the theatre called Around the Greenwood Tree
We'll be back home by six and have fish and chips for tea.

Don't panic I'm fine, I know where I am
I've had time to think while we're stuck in this traffic jam
When the traffic moves again I'll follow the correct sign,
You may think I'm lost but I assure you that we're fine
We're on the A 27 not far from Nottingham
I've studied the maps and so I know where I am
You're driving this car and you know where you are
We could be in Scotland we've already travelled so far

We've been travelling six hours and the kids have been naughty
We're now two hundred miles from home
And Nottingham was only forty
Call yourself a driver, your sense of direction is crap
Pull into this lay by and give me that blooming map

This road goes to Portsmouth not Nottingham you dope
To get to the theatre by two we haven't got a hope
We're getting a satnav, if and when we get back
And as our family driver you're getting the sack
It's twelve in the morning we'll be in Rotherham by five
And first thing tomorrow I'm learning how to drive

It's a warning to all men if you take out the car
And the family are with you, never go very far
But if the nagging persists and becomes quite a pain
Then please stay at home and send them off by train
The moral of this story and a lesson for life
When you go on a long journey please don't take your wife.

Rotherham to Portsmouth is 219 miles

Oh I Do Like to be Beside the Seaside

It's a wonderful experience to paddle in the sea
And see ships on the horizon I've counted twenty three
Sitting in a deck chair on the golden sands and reading a favourite book,
Whilst ladies pass by in bikinis and I'm pretending not to look.

The wife suggests an ice cream in fact a ninety nine
I stroll along the beach to buy some and the weather it is fine
The ice creams start melting and I'd better eat mine quick
The wife's ice cream starts to dribble so I give it a crafty lick

The kids are back from playing and want an ice cream too
If the wife was not with me I'd tell them what to do
After refreshments I take the kids down to the sea as I've been told
They try to get me to swim with them but it's too blooming cold.

Back to the amusements and get to stay there for a while
I've wasted six pound fifty and the wife gives me a smile
The kids are tired and hungry so I ask them what they wish
We want sit on a bench near the harbour wall
And eat some chips and fish

The day out is now over and we leave Scarborough once again.
How I wish we could travel home on a LNER steam train
But it's past York and Tadcaster and down the A1 for us
But today thank goodness I'm not driving, we've travelled there by bus.

The Sea

The sea was both cruel and kind
The frightful time long ago
Deafening sounds and flashing lights penetrated the dark sky
As hour upon hour they marched
Like a never-ending stream through war torn streets
Where swarms of people covered the sandy beach
Back and forth, those gallant boats went
Through a sea of grey, red and black
Strewn with debris and bodies drifting to watery graves
The sand was silent
Littered with broken souls that breathed no more
While across the sea with deafening sounds and flashing lights gone
Many lay safe upon the sand, silently waiting and praying
And covering the sandy beach in England's pleasant land.

*This poem is very special and was written by a good friend and
a talented lady called Carol Walsh. She was a member of a creative
writing group and this poem has always been special to me.*

Albert the Bogus Architect

Albert Tanner was an architect and planned a new estate
He always liked a challenge and something to create
He wanted shops and ten bus stops and put them on his plan
He designed some lanes and public drains, from his mobile caravan
His plans complete showing every street, our Albert was the best
So to the pub to get some grub, then off home for a rest

Now Albert had a secret that he kept from his boss Big Tony
He'd never done this job before and his references were phony
Now Tony was amazed at him and made a song and dance
For Albert was a likable chap and he gave him a second chance
If Hilda the builder a friend of mine, likes this estate you've planned
When designing your next project I'll give you a helping hand

He met with Hilda, the lady builder and showed her what he had done
She looked at Albert with his tablet, and said, where are the houses my son?
He dropped his tablet did our Albert, and said, how could I have forgotten
Because at this job, you are all gob, and at designing estates you're rotten
So he made up his mind and resigned, and went back to his previous trade
Of selling maps to well off chaps, in London town near Horse Guards Parade

Cardboard on Your glasses

Kenneth take off those glasses, you do look a disgrace
The cardboard you've taped to them, looks like blinkers
That horses wear in a race.
But they are my new invention says Ken and they are rather fun
And my only intention is to shade my eyes from the sun

That is the reason that I've put these side pieces on,
So that I can read my book you see
One thing is certain that if you draw the curtain,
The sun won't shine in your eyes,
Or instead you could move to the settee.

But Ken stayed where he was
Determined and eating a piece of toffee
And after getting some stick,
Ken jumped up quick
And spilled his cup of coffee.

It took him an hour to clean up the mess,
Midst ranting and raging from his wife
She was so mad at him that day,
That he barely escaped with his life

A warning to men, who like our Ken,
And read with the sun in their eyes,
Don't stick Card to your glasses
Or you may be in for a surprise

Go into the kitchen and make some tea
And don't read your book at all
But if you really must, despite your wife's disgust
Then go and read your book in the hall

Now his wife feeling smug and without apparent cause
Spilled her own cup of coffee on Ken's chest of drawers
Inside each drawer it was wet and had to be dried out
With J cloths and man size tissue
Ken was having a ball as he watched it all
And read his book now that his glasses
With card sides were no longer an issue

Ben and Santa Clause

Santa Clause is coming, his mother said to Ben
Just watch one more programme and be in bed by ten
I'll put a drink and mince pies out for Santa about half past eleven
Now Ben knew it was his dad from about the age of seven

It happened two days before Christmas before he got into bed
He looked out of the window and saw dad sneak into the garden shed
Early the following morning just before seven O clock
Ben went to the shed with key in hand and opened up the lock

And on the bench piled high and also on the floor
Were things he'd ask Santa for and in fact quite a few more
Now Ben was a clever kid and from that day never said a word
He suspected he wouldn't get as much if his parents ever heard

Now Ben kept up this pretence until he was nearly twelve
After seeing his dad in a Santa suit and his mother dressed like an elf
He recognised them as they spoke and he gave them such a fright
He asked them what they were doing in the middle of the night

They said they loved playing Santa and dressed like this each year
They came down stairs every Christmas morn for mince pies and some
beer
They carried on this tradition until Ben was twenty when he joined in
the fun
On that final time they celebrated for on that day Ben was twenty one

The Treasures in My Garage

Don't throw that wood away I'll need it sometime soon
And save those Jam jars for me love and that old wooden spoon
Jars come in useful for keeping screws and filling full of paint
When she sees how many jars I've got it'll make her feel quite faint

My garage is full of useful things that I have had for years

I've got thirty screwdrivers, and a bike that has no gears
When I can't find a tool I need I go and buy another
My wife says that if I was organised I wouldn't need to bother

I have so many jobs I've started on a bench I made of wood
There are wooden toys and jigsaws with pictures of Robin Hood
There's dozens of Christmas ornaments in all stages of production
But without this sort of challenge I certainly wouldn't function

I've a workshop full of everything, who could want for more?
From scroll saws, jig saws, coping saws, every kind of saw,
Jack planes, smoothing planes, shoulder planes and planes without a
blade
Firmer chisels, bevelled edge and mortice chisels most types they ever
made

Cordless drills, hand drills, electric drills and even a brace and bit
Try squares, mitre squares adjustable squares on racks where they all
can fit
All these are the treasures I have to help me with my many tasks
But the greatest treasure is my wife, and I make everything she asks

Willy Oxley's Clock

Willy Oxley's daughter Jean
The fairest girl in Shire Green
Attracted boys from everywhere
As she visited dance hall and local fair

Romance offered and Jean was glad
Until her new boyfriend met her dad
Jean sat there in her new pink frock
And father began to wind the clock
Jean knew that he was not suited
As out of the door this lad was booted

Willy Oxley's daughter Jean
On the boys was always keen
Whilst voting at a local election
She met a lad who worked in vivisection

He asked her out Oh what a joy
Until he turned up as a Teddy Boy
With long black jacket and crepe sole shoes
And drainpipe trousers how could he lose
This real cool Ted was extremely glad
Until the clock was wound up by her dad

Willy Oxley's daughter Jean
An average early fifties teen
Went through boyfriends which made her sad
Should she hide that blooming clock from her dad

She failed with Brian, Stan, Eric, Bill and Jack
Who after meeting dad never came back
Disillusioned and almost without hope
Until she met dashing Maurice Cope
His first meeting with dad gave Jean a shock
When Maurice admired her father's clock

Willy Oxley's daughter jean
With figure like a beauty queen
Gave her dad a friendly smile
As he whisked her down the aisle

Maurice was her perfect man
And they honeymooned in a caravan

Two children came and her joy overflowed
At a semi detached on a Kimberworth Road
When the lads brought home girls they received a shock
For Jean had inherited her father's clock

Holidays in Whitby

I went to Whitby as a young lad
With my brothers and sister,
And our dog Mandy and me mam and dad.
We went there in a Cooperative van
Driven by Dennis who was a lovely man

It took us over five hours to get us there
We went the long way round to be fair
Past Bridlington and Filey and Scarborough too
We landed in Whitby about half past two

We went to Whitby our aunty for to see
She lived in a bungalow overlooking the cold North Sea
We spent time on the beach every day
We went in the sea and had games to play
We'd saved up our money for to spend every day
I went to the park and the archery range which was on my way
And spent a good amount of money shooting arrows on the grass
And then past the famous whale bones and to the Khyber Pass.

My family played the slot machines at penny a go
In days before decimal coinage, real money you know
Then a walk round old Whitby and have a good look
At the house where once there lived the famous Captain Cook

I used to visit the harbour with sketchbook in hand
Or sit in a deck chair and sketch on the sand
I'd draw St. Margaret's church and the famous Abbey too
When you enjoy yourself like this the days are too few

Aunt Elsie showed us all round that town until our feet were so sore
And when I learned to drive we visited Whitby once more

Ronald Town

We visited local places like Grosmont and Sandsend
We loved our time there and wished our holidays wouldn't end

Over the years we've visited Whitby on countless day trips
And always visited the old town for lunch and eaten fish and chips
My parents and Aunty are sadly no longer here with us today

But memories of those holidays are here with us to stay.

Bikes in the fifties

(memories from my childhood)

In the nineteen fifties my brother and myself and our friends on the street
all under ten years of age had never ridden a bike and one of our neighbours Glyn who was much older than us gave us a small red bike and half the kids on the street learned to ride on that bike. This was at a time when there were probably half a dozen cars on the estate and safe for kids back then.

When we were in secondary school a friend of my dad's called Jack,Shepherd gave us a monster of a bike weighing what seemed like half a ton.

On one occasion in the school holidays we decided to go to Greasbrough dams I rode the bike a few hundred yards along Kimberworth Park road and left the bike for the next person to come along and he did the same. Somehow six of us lads arrived in Greasbrough with the bike, having all ridden it.

Later on when a number of us had bikes of our own we rode to Wentworth,
Elsecar and beyond.

Once I had a Hercules bike for Christmas and remember riding it to the local shops and forgetting about it until I got home and that was the last that I saw of my bike.

She Knows Her Onions

Now Betty knows her onions better than James May knows his cars
This year she had so many onions she's fill more than forty Jars
They are to a secret recipe that we suspect contains some sherry

After only four pickled onions last Friday, Marion felt quite merry
After four more onions Betty knew she'd really gone too far
And after keeling over in her front room, Colin carried her to the car

Now this situation cannot continue with ladies being canned
So Ron got up a petition to get pickled onions banned
It was signed by all Betty's neighbours and people at the shops
Who believed that the secret ingredient was, not sherry but hops
Now Chris and Malcolm became angry at the thought of no more onions
Chris used them to help him sleep at night
And Malcolm put them on his bunions

Now some of the walking group were livid for they had become addicted
After eating a jar of onions they became noisy, and close to being evicted
Others admitted drowsiness and other strange sensations
Like imagining Ron with a full head of hair and other hallucinations
Now Karen had the answer, to these strange happenings, which she knew to be risky
And told Betty to use all vinegar next year, and not fifty percent whiskey

Two Pianists are Better Than One

There's an ensemble in church that have played there for years
Through much adversity heartache and tears
The reason for this trouble I'd better explain
It's because of the burden placed on poor Ron and poor Jane
They're often accused of playing flat and also out of tune
By no other person than the bullying Church pianist June

70 years at the piano you may think it is false
But our June can play Chopin's famous minute waltz
She plays is so fast her fingers begin to smoke
Well that's what she told me but I think it was a joke
She had so many lessons to learn to play proper
Once she gets going even Peter cannot stop her

She's played in this church for almost six decades
And more often than not she gives us all headaches
But joking apart we'd be lost without her playing
She's a consummate artist that goes without saying
She's played every hymn from Wesley, Kendrick and Getty
She once played a chorus by a woman called Betty

Who picked these words and this blooming awful tune?
I bet it's that Steve or Ron said our pianist June
If we hear that song once more it'll drive us all crazy
I know who's to blame it's from Peter's song book from Taize
Whoever's at fault she'll grumble behind their back
And it's always me and Jane who gets all the flack

There are times when on purpose I'll choose a new song
Just to see her face when the music it goes wrong
But to give her credit she carries on and perseveres
She gets her own back and leaves us all in tears
For she drowns out the whistle and guitar and causes us pain
It's her way of saying to us don't do that again

There's many a thing that the congregation don't see
When we all start to play music in the totally wrong key
But it's remedied by June as per her instruction
Give them a smile and make out it's a fancy introduction
When June's not too pleased with me she'll bang on the piano
But I ignore her completely and stare at the banner

Now Junes been poorly and can't see the music too well

And Doreen's taken over and at the piano does excel
But history repeats itself and she's just another June
She waits while we've started and changes the tune
Now Jane and I get our own back and we're now feeling smug
While Doreen's not looking we pull out the plug

Now we both are feeling guilty now Doreen's off sick
So back to June we grovel and that does the trick
Now June's back at the piano and fondles the keys
She strokes it quite gently and looks very pleased
Now June's like the piano and both of them are grand
She's making a special come back as I understand
But she's warned me and Jane to keep in time with her playing
But Jane's reply to her I'd rather not be saying

Benjamin Bumble

Some people are obsessed with cars and some like antique Chairs
Some collect stamps or coins or books but I like all kinds of bears
I discovered an ancient book one day in a bookshop behind the stairs
I found the description of a magic land ruled by a race of bears
It contained a map did that old book which showed the way to go
I at once set out upon my quest though it was thick with snow

I walked upon unfamiliar paths among the cliffs by the sea
When I sensed a change in atmosphere as strange as strange can be
I walked through a magic cave beneath the golden sand
And found myself still walking in a strange new wonderland
I came upon a creature all covered in golden hair
To my surprise I had happened upon a magic talking bear.

It welcomed me with open arms and invited me to go
Into that land of plenty where it did not rain or snow
Up to his house we sauntered for a meal beyond belief
Every good thing I like to eat including potted beef.
A mirror stood upon a wall I found which caused me to stare
I entered that land a lean young man but now I was a bear

In a land without concern about money, stocks and shares
I lived life to the full among those talking bears
I lived out my fantasy in that land so lavish and so green
I saw wonders that no other man or woman had ever seen
Wonderful giant fruit trees and fields full of wheat

And everyone in that land had always plenty to eat.

I lived in that fair land for many a long year
In time I became king you'll be glad to hear
And was known by the name King Benjamin Bumble
And lived in a palace right next to the Jungle
I ruled that land with joy and compassion
A land where my flares were always in fashion

One day while walking with that first friend called Dave
I rediscovered the path that led to the cave
I came out into a land still covered in snow
A place I remembered from so long ago
I then discovered something that made me so sad
I was now once again a young and handsome Yorkshire lad.

Life was back to normal if not a little sad
But I still remembered the best years that I'd ever had
No time had passed whilst I'd been away
And the very next year we went to Scarborough to stay
And once again fate played a hand and I rediscovered that magic cave
And I was transformed once again and met my old friend Dave

Now every two years I went back home again
To see my mates in Rotherham and travelled there by train
And went back to my fantasy land where no time had passed at all
And throughout my teenage years I certainly had a ball
But like the kids in Narnia I grew too old to be their king
But my memories of being a bear what joy it did bring
I remembered that land with the seaside entrance and exit
And thou I'm 72 I'm going back there again to that land
With no rain and snow and never a mention of Brexit

The Present Dilemma

What Can I buy for Christmas it gets more difficult each year
I always buy my cousin Glenn several cans of beer
Most people buy me chocolate, books and some real ale
My wife says don't spend money now but wait for the January sale

Most people we know have everything they need
At Christmas and birthdays too.
And I look down my Shopping list not knowing what to do
I go around the shops each year, in a kind of haze
Until I realise on Christmas Eve that I've now run out of days

This year we're not buying presents and I know that it's not funny
The easy option is a gift token or give them all some money
Writing Christmas cards each year gives me writer's cramp
I'm only handing out cards this year because I can't afford the stamp

Michael's Famous Shed

Michael neighbour and a friend built himself a shed
Inside he put a chest freezer and a double bed
A microwave, a bottle fridge and a coloured telly
And family come to visit them including Aunty Nelly

The shed is built on decking as large as a tennis court
It's famous in our neighbourhood as a work of art
The shed is an iconic structure and folks come from far and near
Not to admire mike's woodwork but his twenty gallons of beer

Deck chairs are out every summer outside this luxurious man cave
With Michael reading his news paper alongside his lovely wife Mave
Now Mavis is drinking brandy and Michael a bottle of beer
Whenever the sun is shining whatever the time of year

Now Michael has a keg of beer and is filling bottles with a funnel
Whilst neighbour Ron is busy working on his tunnel.
Now Ron doesn't sleep much and rarely goes to bed

And his tunnel's is now completed alongside Michael's shed

Now when he looks through his window and sees a party going on
He runs straight through his tunnel
Knowing there's a hot dog and a drink for Ron
He's lucky to have such good neighbours
Who makes him welcome every year
And have similar hobbies to him, eating food and drinking beer

Now NASA built the Hubble telescope and there is nothing finer
From space they can see the earth and the Great Wall of China
But last year a new object was spotted by an astronaut called Fred
Was it an island or a pyramid, no it was Michaels famous shed
They sent experts to Kimberworth, shed and decking for to measure
It is now in all the guide books as our latest national treasure

The Walking Frame Race

Now walking frames are popular among a certain age group today
You can get them free from the council but others have to pay
They come in all sorts of shapes and sizes and different colours too
The one I prefer above all the rest is in a shade of blue

Last week in the church hall on Kimberworth Park
Two ladies with walking frames had a race
Around the church hall thirty times, until Doreen was blue in the face
Geraldine was in front, by lap thirty two and then she said no more
They came to a halt by the serving hatch and called the race a draw

Now Derek and Ron had been looking on and it was a sight to see
And to keep them both from laughing they made a cup of tea

Now the whole congregation had been watching
And gave a mighty cheer
Then Geraldine and Doreen shouted out as one
It's someone else's turn next year

Tooth Hurty

My too hurts so bad, so I visit the dentist today
That tooth must come out sir, it's full of decay
Four injections in my gum, I want to scream and shout
Then with pliers and other tools he starts to pull it out
The tooth is cracked and comes out in bits
I'm at the point of having fits

A few more pulls and the job is done
The dentist sighs and the battles is won
In goes the wadding to stop the bleeding
In the waiting room the notices I'm reading
Back in the chair my mouths now OK
Cool drinks and soup for the rest of the day

My toothache has gone no and more pain
The anaesthetics worn off I'm hurting again
 My gums are sore and so are my lips
I could really murder some fish and chips
Not any old fish but at least a battered Shark
My mouth back to normal and I'm thankful for
Those brilliant dentist's on Kimberworth Park

Is There a Squirrel in the Garden?

There's a squirrel in our garden my wife shouts to me
It's running along the fence now it's climbing up the tree
I come to the window and plenty of birds do I see
I can't understand it for no squirrel do I see
It's in the top right had corner behind that yellow leaf
Why I can't see it too almost beggars belief

Now this is not the first time this has happened
With squirrels and with all kind of birds
To explain my predicament I cannot find the words
It's the same when I'm driving my wife sees a lot
Of things on our journey, all things that I do not
I think that I need medication perhaps some Epsom salts
She's also the only one who can see my many faults

In future when she sees a squirrel I'll pretend I also see
That furry little animal climbing up our tree
I know that this is wrong agreeing with my wife
But it is the only way I know to make a peaceful life
But I've just thought of something,
What if the squirrel which on our fence it did not run
And it was my wife's secret way of fooling me and also
having fun

Pits and the Tally Man

Many men down our way worked at local pits
Hewing coal with a pick and breaking it to bits
They worked at Roughwood and Manvers,
Barley Hole and Cortonwood
In the days before health and safety,

When pit props were made of wood
My own dad worked at Aldwarke, at Silverwood and Cadeby too
In the forties and fifties there was not much else to do

Many men on Kimberworth Park
Worked in mines or steelworks around the Town
And were paid in cash on Fridays in packets that were brown
Life for their wives was hard in those far off days
They were always short of cash
For many men on Friday nights off to the pub did dash
The women were given housekeeping and not too much I fear
And many men spent all their wages on cigarettes and beer

Clothes and other necessities were often bought on tick
Paid back at a few shillings every week to a Tally Man called Nick
Around our way this was called paying on the never-never
For the payments to these debt collectors seemed to go on for ever
Christmas time was worst for after buying toys, food and beer
The Tally Man was laughing for you paid for this all year
There were good times too in those days that now seem so remote
In days when neighbours helped each other all being in the same boat

The steelworks have all but gone and we now buy coal from abroad
And people work at many jobs but there are things families can't afford
And the Tally Man is seen no more and many use payday loans
For debt is still a major problem in many people's homes
Many today are better off than parents and grandparents too
It both partners are earning money and are careful what they do
The secret of my debt free life is if you can't afford it don't buy it
That new car or carpet can wait, see it my way and try it

Not all families lived on credit in the fifties but for those with a number of children it was difficult to survive on housekeeping. In those days in many working class households the man kept what was left after he gave his wife her housekeeping money which she was expected to feed and clothe her family

Happy Days as Kids on Kimberworth Park

They say that you often look upon your childhood through rose coloured spectacles, a time when it never rained and much of life was happy and carefree. Other people around then may remember things slightly different but these are my memories as I recall them.

Ronald Town

As told in the previous poem life was hard for most working class parents but at the time most kids were oblivious to this, it was how things were, and they reveled in the freedom of a new house surrounded by fields and woods.

Living on a new housing estate in the early nineteen fifties for young kids was a dream play ground and after the builders finished for the night the kids were everywhere under floors and on scaffolding and even on roofs. My spending money was three pence or six pence, sixty five years on and memory fades. Some things you will always remember and I include some in this short piece.

Building sites after working hours were an attractive playground for us with piles of sand to play on. One major attraction was to collect the Ben Shaws pop bottles the builders had left which we could take back to Jim Bayliss's paper shop on St. John's Green next day and get fourpence on each bottle. We made quite a bit of money in days when fish, chips and sloppy peas at Webb's chippie was one shilling. *(They are now called mushy peas).* I heard recently that some kids climbed over the back wall of the shop at night and next day took the bottles back for a second time. Honestly it wasn't me.

We climbed onto the scaffold when Wellfield lodge was being built and removed the builder's line for our bow strings and were chased along Kimberworth Park Road by the local bobby. We often had groceries delivered by the Co-op by a van driver called Dennis and the box was tied up with string that we also used for bow making. The arrow flights were made from cereal boxes cut into a heart shape and inserted into a slit cut into the arrow.

We played for hours with homemade bow and arrows which were really powerful. We also made throwing arrows which were about ten inches long and launched using a knotted string. They could travel from Byrley Road to where the church is now.

Dangerous toys are banned today but we never had an accident in all the years that we played with them. Even conkers are banned in schools.

We spent hours at the raft pond where Jewitt Road was built and our flimsy homemade rafts would be a health and safety nightmare today.

We also played at the Lilly Pond on Lord Oaks Lane or tried fishing at the Engine Ponds behind the Colin Campbell Pub at Kimberworth. There were stories about one of the Engine Ponds having a bottomless shaft and there being pike in another, these were exaggerations but we believed them back then.

On particular day a large trailer was parked on Burgen Road and it was full of large propane or Calor gas bottles. There were about twenty kids milling around until someone released the handbrake and the trailer went down the road over the pavement and into the garden's on Kimberworth Park Road.
Of course to us they looked like bombs and we thought that there would be an explosion and for the next hour or so there wasn't a kid to be seen anywhere.

Lorries collected top soil from a massive pile where the clinic and library once stood and took it to form garden's at newly built homes. They sometimes gave my brother Les and me rides in the lorry between journeys. What would health and safety and risk assessment have to say to this today?

During the building of the church in nineteen fifty seven and fifty eight, my brother and I were on our door step on Byrley Road and witnessed a whirlwind where the rear double fire doors are now. It lifted a wheel barrow and other building materials into the air. I remembered this during the church's sixtieth celebrations and wondered if I had imagined it until Les told me the same thing a few days afterwards.

Every three months we had a large delivery of coal which was part of dad's wages. Every house has a coal place and boards were fitted behind the door jamb to retain the coal.
Because dad would be at work the family mucked in to cart the coal from the road into the coal place.

When we moved in to our new house the only provision for cooking food was on the Yorkshire type range. Mum loved this oven and missed this when we fitted a two ring gas burner and eventually a Parkinson Cowen Cooker with overhead grill. Mum and Grandma said that baking bread was never the same when we got rid of the range. Nothing can replace the joy of putting your feet on the hearth before an open fire.

Kimberworth Park Farm or to give it its proper title Abdy Farm still existed until 1960 when it was demolished to make way for the Domino Public House which was opened in December 1961. This was adjacent to what became Redscope School, named after Redscope Plantation, part of which can still be seen behind the football field behind the school.

The writer and other school children who attended Redscope School would purchase orange juice from the farmer's wife at the cost of 3d per glass.

You can read about Abdy Farm in Jeannette Hensby's book, The Abdy Farm Murders. A sad but interesting book which I highly recommend.

Until Redscope Juniors was built kids of my age attended Thornhill Junior School.

When Redscope School was finally built we left Thornhill school and started in a brand new school. We must have been some of the only children in the country who attended brand new schools for most of their school lives for in 1958 we were first years at the brand new Old Hall School which I was informed was the first Secondary School to wear School uniforms.

We sometimes helped ourselves to pears from the trees behind the farmhouse and luckily we were never caught. There is still an apple tree in the Chislett car park that may have been from the old farm.

The barns were alongside what is now the path to the Chislett and when they were demolished around 1960 we carried many of the large roof timbers onto the field in front of our house on Byrley Road for bonfire night nineteen sixty.

The bonfire was so big the embers burned for almost a week after bonfire night. We kids saved our pocket money up for weeks before bonfire night and just before the event went to the old inside market on Domine Lane and spent the whole of it on penny bangers. Bonfire nights on the new estate were occasions for the whole family and we looked forward to it for months. The smell of wood smoke, jacket potatoes and bonfire toffee still bring fond memories of these happy times. The only accident that I remember was a firework landing in someone's wellington but no serious damage was done.

Where Kimberworth Park Road meets Oaks Lane there was a row of very old pit houses on Pepper Alley and when they were demolished many of the residents were re-housed in Kent Road. Many of the men were friends of dad and every Sunday morning walked across the fields to the Effingham Arms which the locals called the Dropping Well. I wonder if the brewery knew this when they renamed the pub The Droppingwell a few years ago?

These are just a few of my memories of the first few years on a brand new estate and others may remember things differently but these are some of the things that I recall today over sixty years later.

Twenty One Again

If I could spend a year as a young man of twenty one
And retain all my memories I'd be a different Ron
I'd become much fitter and do all the things I like
And once again go cycling on my racing bike

I'd have a healthier lifestyle and cut down on eating chips
And when on holiday in Whitby I'd go on sailing ships
I'd walk more miles each week and travel less by car
I'd become slimmer during that year and healthier by far

I'd spend my money wisely during that extra year
And save more for the future and also drink less beer
I'd appreciate my family and friends more than I did before
I'd help mum with the household chores and often sweep the floor

I'd dress myself more wisely as experience has told me to
I'd wear smarter clothing and a better style of shoe
I'd save up for a hair transplant and try to impress my mates
But I fear I'd become a person that everyone now hates

I'd remember my future life and not make the same mistakes again
But they say that history repeats itself and that is such a pain
I can't go back and change things and I don't think that I should
I've a lovely wife, family and friends and my life right now is good

My Shiny Beanie Hat

I have a hat with a light on, I wear it every night
My friends are all amazed; they never thought I was that bright
It is a fleece my hat is, and keeps my head so warm
I bought it from a travelling man at a local farm

The man I bought my hat from was a smashing fellow
He invented it whilst working in a cold and draughty cellar
He wanted both hands free for lifting cardboard boxes
Full of out of code bananas for feeding local foxes

These hats are now so popular they sell them in the streets
To all evening joggers and policemen on their beats
They are now replacing standard lamps in many people's houses
People wear them standing up in living rooms wearing yellow trousers

We wear ours on Tuesday nights when it is dark and dim
For planting seed potatoes and bringing the washing in
My friends all think I'm crazy with this hat upon my head
For I wear it everywhere I go and even in my bed

Different coloured lights are available and used on Friday nights
People stand in them on country lanes and replace the traffic lights
I wear mine as a fashion statement and love all kinds of flattery

But my ego took a hammering last week when I had to replace the battery

My Balanced Diet

I always have my five a day said Malcolm to his mate
Unless it's fruit and vegetable for these I really hate
I have five Yorkshire puddings with my Sunday Dinner
And chips and five eggs for breakfast will always be a winner
For lunch I have five muffins and if I'm hungry I have five more
Then I'm often in trouble, for leaving crumbs upon the floor
I have five bacon sandwiches at the local caff
I eat them standing on my head and make all the customers laugh
On Friday night I have chips and five fish which is a local tradition
I eat them from a dustbin lid at a table in our kitchen
But if I'm really truthful I eat an apple on the quiet
I do this on a Saturday as part of my balanced diet.

The Tai Chi Group of St. John's Church

(The Tai Chi group finished ran for four years and finished in 2017)

The Tai Chi group at St. John's church what a sight to see
The ages range is from fifty one to over ninety three
They begin with their arms out stretched and wriggle both their hands
Like an ancient airplane just before it lands.

With David Barrow out in front to guide us in our task
This is our weekly exercise if anyone should ask
Kick out your feet, lean to the side and hands upon your knees
You'd be amazed to see the looks we get from Doreen and Denise

It's good for the heart our David says, it keeps your blood pressure down
That's fine with me we hear a shout from St. John's young Ron Town
We have a short break before we start our very special exercise
And to see us twist our bodies so comes as a big surprise

We improve our balance and heart rate as we step out young and old
All types of people join us, grey haired, no hair and some with hair of gold
In our group we also have our ex-Mayor and Kath his lovely wife.
We all get our life blood flowing at Tai Chi for a better quality of life

When we've done our movements for over half an hour
We feel tingling in both our hands and feeling of great power
On the stroke of three we all sit down and no longer feel like old codgers
Tea and coffee is welcome now and a plate of Jammy Dodgers

We come along each week all throughout the year
The only thing that's missing is a lovely glass of beer
We must be David's favourite group the one and only number one
For we are the geriatric Tai Chi group at Kimberworth Park, St. John

The Famous Yorkshire Highland Games

No one today remembers the famous Yorkshire Highland Games
Opened in fourteen twenty seven by Duchess Geraldine James
The games took place in Rotherham on large green piece of land
Known today as Masbrough next to Bradgate Sands.
The first game was won by Sheila Ann a Lady of ill repute
It's not what you are thinking but for eating liquorice root
That famous sight enhancer when arrows she did shoot
She won by shooting half a mile and hitting a leather boot

Next the spear throwing event won by a man named Smith
Who threw his spear up Wortley Road and landed in a cliff
He was almost disqualified for breaking the Highland code
For throwing his spear out of bounds and across a busy road
Now Kickball the next event between teams from near and far
The final match was between two teams from Swinton and Bessacarr
The winning goal was scored by a seven foot Swinton man called Chris
Who filled the trophy full of Whisky and muttered "this is bliss".

Next the long distance road race from
All Saints Church to Manor Barn

It began on the stroke of midnight and ended with the dawn
The runners were tired and weary and a good night's sleep did lack
The race should have been a doddle
But not with a sheep upon your back
It was won by a man called Derek a giant from Rotherham
But he had an unfair advantage for on his back he carried a lamb
The judges consulted the rule book which was carved in a rock face
And found that no rules had been broken and Derek won the race

The rock throwing contest was next event and people thought it grand
They threw three pound stones the length of Bradgate Park
Which landed in the sand
They threw on a Wednesday afternoon and had to be done by three
For the judges were strict in this regard
And never missed their afternoon tea

The winner of this rock throwing game came as quite a surprise
It was won by a big lass called Denise
With strong arms and bright blue eyes
She won a year's supply of whole grain bread
And meat from the local butcher
She opened a local sandwich shop
And on prices no one could touch her

The next event was wrestling and the ladies were on first
And drank a pint of beer between each round for to quench their thirst
The first match of that day was won by a stocky lass called June
Who after winning twenty rounds on her lute she played a lively tune
She wobbled around in circles and her sons for her life did fear
But a doctor examined her and said, don't worry
It's the effect of twenty pints of beer
They changed the rules straight away on June and her son's behalf
After every round in future they'll only be drinking half

Men's wrestling was the next event and this caused some alarm
A man called Jack was disqualified for biting his opponent's arm
A man called David took his place and the crown knew he'd go far
For after every round he won he'd strum on his guitar
His opponent was a man called William to the crown was known as bill
And after only two and a half minutes he became noticeably ill
David was announced as the winner and the crowd gave him a cheer
William's illness was a fallacy for he had been drinking so much beer

The games ended on a Friday night and what a celebration
For all the contestants were invited and their numerous relations
A special place was built to celebrate this Yorkshire Highland Games
And the guest of honour was no other than Duchess Geraldine James
The venue was the Manor Barn which is with us still today
But it's no longer tuppence for a pint, three pounds almost to pay
The rounds were paid for by Chris from Swinton
That well known Rotherham son
But he borrowed the money from a mate of his
A gullible man called Ron

Train Spotting Again

Spotting on Doncaster station on a cold winter's day
In search of that elusive loco this is why we stay
But it's more than spotting trains that keeps so many there
It's a hobby from our childhood and memories we often share
For many it started in the fifties with an attraction of all things steam
With some it's the Deltics and other diesels that they dream
But whatever your motive is that brings you back here again
We all agree that there's nothing like the British railway train

Tuesdays and Thursdays are the days on which spotter gather here
No matter what the weather's like or even the time of year
About fifty gather on these days to mainly see the freight
And a coffee or beer with like minder people I find it simply great
I go with mates from Rotherham and we often have a laugh together
Talking about programmes on the telly we forget about the weather
Open All Hours is a favourite, and Peter Kay's funny Car Share
Hello, Hello is another, and Dad's Army's also there

We've visited dozens of stations in this previous year or more
To see steam trains and diesel electrics the numbers I'm not sure
At Carlisle and Worth Valley we went to see some steam
To visit there in my childhood would have been a dream
To go there with my special mates has always been a treat
Especially at the stations that have pasties we can eat
But a bonus attraction to our spotting we can enjoy once again
Is seeing the English countryside as we love travelling there by train

Around the World by Tandem

(Maurice a special friend and I used to joke about going to Argentina in a tandem with a massive snorkel
to allow us to travel under the sea. We decide that the snorkel would be too large)
This poem is written in his memory)

Maurice and Ron decided to cycle across the world nonstop
But no suitable bicycle could be bought from any cycle shop
So the two inventive geniuses put their heads together
And invented the land and sea quad tandem, made for any kind of weather

Now the friends were excited about their venture and could not be keener
And after discussion with the mayor, their destination was Argentina
This was just over seven thousand miles away on a straight line on the maps
But with most of the journey there by sea they were sure to have mishaps

So they discussed their route in detail through the remainder of that day
And decided to leave from Blackpool and land in Canada's Goose Bay
They set out from Rotherham Town Hall with a handshake from the Mayor
John Foden was the mayor's name and well known to this valiant pair

They cycled for two days to Blackpool and had lunch near that famous Tower
On Harry Ramsden's fish and chips which they ate for over half an hour
With floats and outboard motor into the Atlantic Ocean the pair sailed away
And to save on precious fuel supply they pedaled for many a day

In a box behind their tandem they kept ready meals in waterproof dishes
And to supplement their diet they often lived on sun dried fishes
They encountered other vessels and sent messages to their wives and others

And discovered they'd been sponsored by friends, sisters and by brothers

They landed in Goose Bay, that year, on December the twenty third
And of their unique Atlantic crossing everyone there had heard
They stayed in people's homes for Christmas had fun the whole day long
And when Ron played carols on his recorder Maurice burst into song

They travelled through Canada; the US and Belize; for almost a full year
Also staying in many peoples' houses living on burgers, pizza and beer
They became world famous; appearing on the news; on film and on TV
And with all this publicity, those modest of men, were as happy as can be

They travelled by sea from Belize to Columbia at the start of the New Year
And when landing on dry land, ten thousand people they did cheer
On Maurice's birthday they signed autographs, for three days in Santa Marta
Glad to be at last on dry land again and out of the salty water

For almost eight months they cycled through Brazil and Bolivia
And Ron said the temperature's way too high I'm glad that we don't live here.
I do miss my wife, said Maurice; it's two years since I've seen her
I agree said Ron, but our journey's almost over, for we're now in Argentina

The donated their bike and belongings to the Argentinean National Museum
And folk travelled many hundreds of miles just for to see them.
They travelled a thousand miles by plane, to Buenos Aires the capital city
And just missed the Olympics on the tele which for them was a great pity

Back at last home to Rotherham to a tumultuous reception
All their families and friends were there to meet them without an exception
Said Maurice to Ron the following day, you may say what you like
I never want to go abroad again or see another blooming bike.

The pair appeared on chat shows and were showered with many gifts
They were asked for autographs in the street; and by strangers in lifts
Their sponsorship money came to thousands and with it they did much good
With some of it Maurice bought a computer and Ron he bought some wood

(The Land and Sea Quad Tandem)

The Bag Lady from Kimberworth Park

Carol has had an addiction for over fifty years
This has caused much heartache and also many tears
She never takes drugs or alcohol so what does she do
She's always buying handbags and she's collected ninety two

She takes her bags to charity shops to make space on her floor
But for every bag she gives away she always buys two more
She's got them from many places from Madrid and Timbuktoo
From Belgium and from Germany just to name a few

They come in every colour, in every shape and every size
She recently won a raffle and guess what was first prize?
Some are so ancient they could be from the Ark
They all belong to Carol the bag lady from Kimberworth Park

She also collects shopping bags and spends a lot of lolly
She's often seen on St. John's Green with her shopping trolley
She is a lovely lady and one who never brags
But she cannot see her TV screen for piles of shopping bags

She was given a new settee last week by a friend called Jean
But with her massive pile of bags most of it is never seen
So drastic action has been taken, says Carol I really must stop
So she's taken fifty shopping bags to a charity shop

A Vicious Circle

There are magpies on the chimney just across the street
They eat all the food put out for other birds to eat
But this morning they were surprised
As the food they began to scoff
Two massive pigeons landed and chased the blighters off

There are pigeons on our greenhouse roof
Watching for food placed on the bird table
And try to eat it up before the other birds are able
But next door's cat came and chased them off the street
And all the other birds now came to eat

There are cats in our garden digging up our plants
We've enough problems with caterpillars
And with slugs and with ants
They also leave their calling cards most foul in every way
But this morning the magpies came and chased the cats away

St. John's Mines

Caves were discovered beneath the grass
On St. John's Green one day
When a tractor driver's large tractor wheels suddenly gave way
He was busy cutting grass near the butcher's shop
And disappeared beneath the ground
And the people from the local shops gathered all around

A JCB was sent for and came and rescued him
That poor unfortunate tractor driver a man by the name of Jim
And as the tractor rose slowly from the ground
The folk there began to realise just what had been found
It was the secret entrance to the lost mines of Kimberworth Park
Mentioned in the Doomsday Book
So they sent for the country's top experts for them to have a look

These mines were written in folk law a thousand years ago
By a cousin of William the Conqueror a man called Eric the slow
These were caves discovered by men quarrying for stone
When building Kimberworth Castle which today is now unknown
These caves went on for quite a way beneath that ancient ground
And in them emerald, and rubies and other precious stones were found

But before the extent of the riches in this treasury so grand
The caves were suddenly sealed by royal decree
And all access to them was banned
Why this drastic action losing this wealth beyond compare
This was a time when superstition ruled and no one would enter there.

There were rumours of a metal creature seen on the very first day
And it terrified all who entered and everyone ran away.
King William heard about this and of losing all these riches
In a land of superstition where men believed in witches
He entered the caves at high noon with an army armed to the teeth
And ten minutes later came out screaming a sight beyond belief

Today all this was seen as bunkum and to be taken with a pinch of salt
So Sally Ann and a team of archaeologists made a modern day assault
Using the latest technology they entered this new found cave
And the ladies from the butcher's shop gave them a friendly wave
And as they ventured deeper in they saw nothing of these riches
No monsters, ghouls or ghosties and certainly no witches

But after only half a mile they gave a startled cry

Ronald Town

And stepping back quickly as an express train went by
They found themselves standing by a platform by a railway station then
And on that station was a clock and the time was half past ten
People will never believe us and think we're as mad as a hatter
For the name upon the station house said welcome to Wassa Matta

They met the local historian as he stepped down from a train
Welcome people from Kimberworth Park he said
So you've arrived here once again
All those years ago, your people weren't prepared for this
And our machines that dug the mines were seen as monsters
That people back then believed did exist
And if they had ventured much further
It would certainly have addled their human brains
Seeing all this technology and especially railway trains
When the party returned back to St. John's Green
They were asked by the crowds what they had seen
They told the crowd that the caves contained no wealth
And came to a dead end almost near Oaks Lane
And they said that the caves were dangerous
And should be sealed up once again

Whilst in Wassa Matta the Archaeologists met up with Ron and Ken
Who were on their annual visit and had got off the train just then
They explained about their discoveries and other entrances to this place
And invited them to come again and give lectures to this strange race
They vowed to keep a secret to what they now had seen
And seal up the new entrance on Kimberworth Park's St. John's Green

They came back as promised and made a number of these trips
And after giving lectures they were fed with fish and chips
The people on St. John's green of this were none the wiser
Apart from Hayley at the butchers shop who is their new meat adviser
They supply Wassa Matta with pork pies and other delicious goodies
And Hayley and the queen of Wassa Matta are now the best of buddies

Thing are now quieter on St. John' Green
And now some buildings have been cleared
For a second entrance to Wassa Matta beneath them was found
Just as Ron and Ken had feared
This was filled with concrete late one night and covered over with grass
Not a sign of this could be seen next day as people walked straight past
Cutting grass on the green today is seen to be much slower
For tractors are not allowed there now
It's just a young girl pushing a hand held lawn mower

I Love My Notebooks

I have a confession to make and it may come as a surprise
I have collected notebooks of every shape and size
I cannot pass a bookshop or stationers too
Without buying a notebook and very often two

My family think I'm crackers and others think so too
I just like new notebooks and I've now got thirty two
Each one has a separate use and in one I write my friend's names
And in two other books I write down all my trains

I write passwords in another book which is pink and blue
And in a brown and yellow book I list thing I have to do
In a thicker book I write meeting notes on a Monday night
I write poems in another until I get them right

I buy posh books from Rymans and select them all with care
You can buy them from Poundland and I have a few from there
My last was from Home Bargains its size it was A4
But what I'll use this new book for I'm not really sure

I've a book that's very thick I write things in all year long
Like numbers names and sketches and things that come along
It's better than a diary and records information too
I'll show it to you to prove that what I say is true

Notebooks are so special when their clean and brand new
I write in them with special pens of which I've quite a few
These are real pens with nibs and with ink
And when the nibs dry up as they do I soak them in the sink

I love all my notebooks and keep them for myself
And keep them all together upon my office shelf
So if you want a hobby that doesn't take up too much space
Start collecting notebooks you can buy them any place

I often look through old books and discover forgotten things
To see a long forgotten name, O what joy it brings
I've a friend who keeps a journal and she now has quite a few
I must go out and buy another notebook and keep a journal too

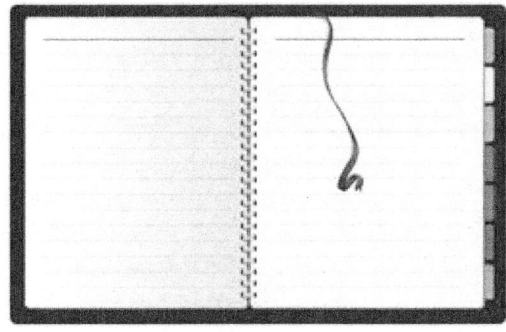

Friends and Neighbours

I knew all my neighbours long ago and this was quite a feat
Most of my mates lived near our house and often we would meet
I don't know all my neighbours like I used to do back in far off days
Some are no longer with us and some have moved away

I remember them with fondness the people on our street
I now have memories of earlier days when often we would meet
Life is like that today and people come and go
But as each year goes by there are fewer that I know

I speak to new neighbours when passing by
And comment about the weather
But I remember neighbours from years ago
When we were all younger then together

But the good news is that I still have neighbours who are friends
Whom I've known for many years
Those I've shared the good time with and also shed many tears
Having good neighbours is a blessing or so I am often told
People who are always there for me are worth their weight in gold
I have many new neighbours now as young as we used to be
And I hope their neighbours become lifelong friends
And bring joy as it has to me.

(Friends from childhood and from later in life God's gifts to us and cannot be bought)

The Passage to Camelot

I found a tree in our local wood the no one else could see
It was planted there by Merlin in five hundred and twenty three
The tree appeared every hundred years on midsummer's night at ten
I happened to be passing through the wood along with my friend Ken
It appeared to us by magic and gave us quite a fright

And after that it appeared to us every Friday night

We found the tree was hollow and without a trace of rot
And as we walked through that tree we entered Camelot
At the sight before our eyes we suddenly became aware
Of none other than the man himself, Merlin standing there.
 He welcomed us like long lost friends and bade come inside
To the legendary world of Camelot and he would be our guide

He explained that we came here by magic to answer his magic call
And when we go back home again no time would have passed at all
He introduced us to King Arthur and other famous nights
And bid Sir Lancelot to show is all the sights
He explained that we had been chosen for a special task
Why we two especially my friend Ken went on to ask

In grief he explained the problem as much as he was able
That King Arthur's knights could never meet without that special table
The table had been damaged by the dastardly Baron Bisket
And no one in King Arthur's realm had the skills to fix it
So Merlin had visited the future to find woodworking men
And quite by chance last Friday night had discovered Ron and Ken

Through that tree we went home again and felt a pair of fools
When we entered the tree next Friday night with our kit of tools
We amazed the Knights of Camelot with our carpentry skills
Especially with our modern glues and our cordless drills
The table was soon fixed and polished, better than new to say the least
And we were hailed as honoured members of the round table
And attended a splendid feast

We often visit on Friday nights but in modesty we never like to boast
That we are famous throughout the land and the object of many a toast
W e have a joiners shop there now and give lessons now and then
I show them how to cut dovetails and drilling holes is shown by Ken
Together we completed a project with those who are now able
And because new Knight are joining we've built a second table

But if you visit our local wood and try to find that tree
You'll have a futile journey for it's only visible

To my friend Ken and me
But in one hundred years on Midsummer's night
As the clock strikes ten
If they're passing through that wood
Your grand kids may see that tree again
Now Camelot may be a myth and King Arthur's knights a fable
But take it from Ken and me for we built their new round table

(Sadly Sir Kenneth of Concord and Sir Ronald of Whitley never made it into the story books)

Little Boxes

Now Ken and I make boxes, we make them out of ply
Solid wood costs a fortune, that's the reason why
We make them any size and shape; and if you think that's funny
We'll make them as big as a suitcase if you have the money

Ken paints his lids with pictures and that is very clear
But sometimes for a change I cover mine with veneer
Birch ply is the favourite for the grain is very straight
Other plies are too brittle and that is what we hate

Butterflies have been popular with folk in past years
But lately owls have replaced them; I think it is the ears
Our boxes are used for many things I'm sure you're glad to know
Some are used for jewellery and others just for show

We make them for our craft group to raise funds every year
And especially in December with Christmas drawing near
So if you want a gift for your daughter husband wife or son
Come along to our craft group and have a word with Ken or Ron

My Posh Meal

We went for a meal today with my family
To a fancy restaurant at about half past three
We all had different starters chosen by our group
I had prawn cocktail and my son had mushroom soup

For the main course I fancied chicken served on a piece of slate
At the price it cost for food here why can't we have a plate
I like chips with everything and they serve them in a dish
So I changed my mind about chicken and ordered chips and fish

For a pudding there was a special menu upon the restaurant wall
I wish I had brought binoculars the writing was so small
I chose death by chocolate with cream that was so thick
I wish I'd had the cheesecake for I'm feeling rather sick
I was suddenly feeling better so I thought that I'd risk it
And have a coffee and a plate of cheese and biscuits
But my wife as per usual has had the final say
Save the cheese and biscuits Ron for another day

The waiter brought the bill for us on a paper Oh so quaint
One hundred and forty pounds it said and left me feeling faint
We had a whip round for the cash as best as we were able
With so much money for our food I thought we'd bought the table

Next time we have a family meal we are never coming here
Well send out for fish and chips and buy supermarket beer
And if we go to a pub for to quench our thirst
We'll never order food again before checking the prices first

The Post Wassa Matta Years

During my fifties and after my many visits to Wassa Matta I decided to embark on something entirely different and so I visited the world famous Swiss singing academy and enrolled on a Alpine horn and yodelling class and in just over six months I became so good that I had my first hit CD entitled four part harmony yodelling in South Yorkshire and for the second time in my life I became world famous.

I was invited to appear on American television with none other than Jane Fonda and Clint Eastwood who remembered me from when I was the world's top male model. All went well until I knocked the host of the show Wally Winkett Junior off of his stool with my thirty foot Alpine horn. Wally was not pleased to say the least and I was asked to leave the studio and told where to put my horn.

I was inconsolable and so Jane and Clint took me to a café and bought me a chocolate drink and a Hamburger. They explained that Wally Winkett hated Yorkshire men after being sold a inferior Yorkshire pudding in Devon England. I explained that they may be good at making clotted cream but only a true Yorkshire person can make Yorkshire pudding.
Jane and Clint sympathised and arranged for me to make a film with them which involved horn playing and yodelling in the Grand Canyon. To promote this venture I recorded a new yodelling song entitled "I remember everyone one else but you" as a tribute to my singing hero Frank Ifield. It made number one in the charts and my fan club manager Maggie sent out half a million signed photographs in the first three months.

Maggie was ill for weeks afterwards from licking all those stamps. I sent her for an extended holiday in Wassa Matta where the top doctor there completely cured her and she became national pin up girl and was invited to many of the biggest events in that land and stayed with Odea Rimee me and her husband.

She came back to Rotherham and gave demonstrations in juggling and fire eating and back flips which she learned in Wassa Matta.
Whilst playing my Alpine horn in the Grand Canyon the vibrations caused a minor landslide and exposed the entrance of a cave which when the dust had settled I entered and received the greatest shock of my life.

In that cave I found amazing artefacts and a hand written journal over a thousand years old. This was undeniable proof that a team of people from Rotherham had landed in America even before the earliest settlers or the Vikings. They had built a fleet of boats from English Hardwoods and sailed there with a crew of one thousand miners whose names were written in the front cover of the book and by some strange coincidence three of the names were ancestors of my good friend Ken, Maggie the juggler and myself.

And on the second page was the original recipe for Yorkshire Pudding.
The rest of the journal outlined their time in America. They had arrived by this stream and started panning for Gold and they began digging deeper and deeper until over a period of years the Grand Canyon was formed. The cave was full of amazing things which would make Tutankhamen's tomb seem plain in comparison. Luckily I was on my own at the time and with some brushwood and bracken covered the entrance to the cave. I realised the no one else would be able to reach the entrance without the help of a thirty foot Alpine horn and a mountain goat.

The following year I returned in my private jet and accompanied by Ken, Dame Maggie, and her good friend Countess Karen. We emptied the cave and returned to South Yorkshire and opened a museum in a secret location on Kimberworth Park and viewing was by invite only. I sent my personal chef to America and she cooked a Sunday lunch complete with Yorkshire puddings for Wally Winkett Junior. He was overwhelmed by the gesture and immediately booked me on to his show along with Maggie who juggled with Yorkshire puddings whilst I yodelled to a version of On Iltley Moor Ba Tat.

Dame Maggie became very wealthy and became involved in voluntary work in the kitchen of a local church and used her skill as a fire eater to cook the bacon for the bacon butties. She was banned from doing back flips in the kitchen for health and safety reasons.
Ken and I had a long earned rest and spent time doing woodwork painting pictures and filling cracks in ceilings.

This did not last for long and the following year Ken and I flew back to the Grand Canyon and entered the cave and uncovered one of the original ships that had come to America and this became headline news. The ship was lifted from the cave by a gigantic crane and is now in pride of place in the Smithsonian Museum in Washington. Another copy if the book was found in the cabin and that is how Kimberworth Park came to be twinned Washington. With the original recipe found in the book, a Yorkshire Pudding shop opened adjacent to the Smithsonian and people travelled many miles to sample this delicacy. Toad in the Hole entered the American language.

Ron and Ken were once again in the world news and were asked to entertain the Senate. Ken played the mouth organ and Karen and I yodelled whilst Maggie did back flips whilst juggling coconuts.

This was made into a DVD and became the top selling DVD of all time. We eventually returned to Rotherham and with the income from DVD sales bought a mansion by the sea and used it as a holiday home in Scarborough for the Local walking group.

Jesus Calms a Storm

Worn out and weary was Jesus and had given the crowds his best
And needed a place of refreshment a place where he could rest
He knew he had to go to a quieter place and had a decision to make
So he got into a boat with his disciples to cross to the far side of the lake
They sailed across that wide lake where the water itself was so deep
And our tired and weary Saviour was soon soundly fast asleep
Suddenly a gale swept across the lake and water engulfed that boat
Whilst Jesus kept on sleeping with his head resting upon his coat
The disciples woke Jesus from slumber as their own fear increased
And as Jesus rebuked the wind and the waves their fury suddenly ceased
Where is your faith said Jesus as the disciples were afraid and amazed
Who is this Jesus that the wind and water obey him?
He is surely someone who ought to be praised

An abundance of Willies

William Green a South Yorkshire man had a family like no other.

For over one thousand years the first son of every male member of the Green family had been given the name William. And many of these had been given a nickname that reflected their personalities or their chosen profession.

His own firstborn went by the name of Willie Teckit because of his propensity to acquire things that belonged to someone else. He never went as far as breaking into houses or stealing purses but if something was left unattended Willie would claim it as his own.

If someone was cutting the lawn and went in for a cuppa Willie Teckit would acquire a lawn mower. In his double garage lock up behind the shops on St. John's Green he had three hundred lawn mowers, two hundred sweeping brushes and a thousand builder's shovels. People became suspicious when the grass on every lawn on Kimberworth Park was over two feet high and Amazon ran out of shovels for sale

All went well until Willie decided to have a garage sale and people from all over the estate came and claimed their possessions. Willie escaped because he had also acquired the lock ups under false pretences. He had cut off the padlocks with a hacksaw. William Green senior sent Willie to their second home in Scarborough for two months until the lawn mower saga had died down. The Scarborough home was paid for by his dad who was a smarter thief than Willie and stole garden gnomes and sold them on Ebay. His nick name was Willie Fisher anmed after the first gnome that he acquired from behind the Colin Campbell pub in Kimberworth.

Willie's cousin from Barnsley was known locally as Willie Eccas Like because whenever he was asked to do something his reply was always will I eccas like. Unlike his thieving cousin, Willie Eccas Like had a proper job. He was chief neb maker for "Flat Caps R Us" in the largest flat cap factory in the world in Barnsley. Willie cut out and stitched on the cap nebs by hand of a thousand flat caps every day. This was in the elite part of the factory where flat caps were all hand made for the famous and the good. Many members of the royal family had flat caps with labels inside the neb saying made in Barnsley by Willie Eccas Like. He was asked to start a factory inside the royal residence at Sandringham but by some strange quirk of nature Willie was allergic to Corgi hairs so he replied in a dignified way will I eccas like your majesties.

In 1654 in a woodcutters hovel on Kimberworth Deer Park lived William Green the 20th Great grand parent of our two Willies. He went under the name of Willie Tellit. He had been handed down the recipe for Yorkshire Pudding by his father Willie fellit the then famous tree feller who met an untimely end when an Oak tree that he was chopping down fell the wrong way and landed on the top of poor him.

Willie Fellit had discovered the recipe for Yorkshire pudding in his youth when working as an apprentice blacksmith and decided to make a pancake for dinner, (nobody had lunch in Yorkshire, dinner was a good enough name for them).

He mixed the batter and put it in a tin mug too near to the furnace while he finished making a chisel for the local carpenter, his cousin Willie Sawitt.

When he went to get his pancake batter he was amazed at what he saw, the very first Yorkshire pudding.

After his early demise his son Willie Tellit decided to open the first café on what would become nearly 400 year later St. John's Green. He made his fortune selling Yorkshire puddings and many, many people asked for the recipe saying to one another will he tell it and his reply was will I eccas like which strangely was his name before inheriting the recipe from his father.

In the early twentieth century lived William Green the grandfather of Willie Teckit and Willie Eccas Like. Willie had inherited a fortune and his time was spent in trying to do impossible things and consequently went by the name of Willie Meckitt.

He tried to climb up Kepple's Column and reached the first opening when someone shouted will he meckitt which caused him to lose his grip and he fell to the ground and broke his little finger. He then decided to abseil from the roof of Wentworth Woodhouse and three quarters of the way down ran out of rope and fell to the ground. Fortunately for Willie a young chambermaid was passing and caught him saving him from serious injury.

In those days being found with a man in your arms meant that they were engaged and so they were married the following June. She always told the story of how Willie had fallen for her in a big way.

Willie Meckitt became famous for being the first person to cycle to Sheffield blindfolded. It took him three months of which eleven weeks were spent in hospital recovering from many falls. Willie Meckitt and Lavender Blue who became Lavender Green had two girls and one boy. The girls were called Dilly and Nelly and of course the boy was Willie Fisher the phantom gnome snatcher,

The first William Green was known as Willie Fletcher who collected the arrows at the Battle of Hastings and actually removed the arrow from King Harold's eye and it is now a family heirloom known only to the family and me.

He collected so many arrows that he sold them in London Town and made enough money to become the first High Sherriff of Nottingham and his second son was named Lincoln Green and gave his name to that famous cloth which one his descendants sold to Robin Hood and his merry men and retired on the money that he made. His name was Willie Fortune.

Reggie Bradshaw's Bread and Jam

Reggie Bradshaw a Barnsley lad
Once went fishing with his dad
He set out his stall by Greasbrough Dam
With bottles of beer and bread and Jam
He cast his line and baited his hook
And started to read his favourite book
His dad was fishing in the deep
And Reggie Bradshaw fell fast asleep
His dad who was known as Sam
Ate young Reggie's bread and Jam
Sam caught fish and was of good cheer
So he also drank poor Reggie's beer

Reggie woke up with an appetite
And sensed that something was not quite right
His dad felt guilty and full of remorse
Saying that their sandwiches had been eaten by a horse
His dad then confessed his evil deeds to his son
Telling Reggie Bradshaw what he had done
His dad a reformed nineteen sixties Hippie
Went into Greasbrough to the chippie
The fish and chips were enjoyed by his lad
Who promptly forgave his greedy dad
Sam being a Yorkshire man and quite thrifty
Charged poor Reggie five pounds fifty

The Annual Harvest Supper

The harvest supper at the church last year
With sixty people waiting eagerly there
The pie and peas were served at last
It was time for this crowd to end their fast
Mint sauce came round for their mushy peas

And sixty pies were polished off with ease

The bingo caller has changed from Jim this year
With Karen in charge we've nothing to fear
She shouted out loud all the fours forty four
And some of the numbers fell on the floor
Blind ninety was called followed by a loud response
Three people had a line and shouted at once

Nineteen pounds is hardly divisible by three
Give us six pounds then each one did agree
The full house was won and the game was complete
And straight away Chris Mason was up on his feet
I'm your new quizmaster he said with a grin
But the bad news is that it was written by Jim

The entertainment over it's time for a chat and a cuppa
While we digest our big harvest supper
And some of us enjoy our enormous cup cake
Bought from the shop for sixty is too many to bake
Members from church and the walking group too
And all of us agree that it's been a good do.

*(The Kimberworth Park Walking for Pleasure group are over fifty
Strong and are based at St. John's Church and enjoy meals and days
out with people from the Church. Members from the group also serve
food at the Friday Coffee Morning. People from the local community
work together for the good of the community and the Harvest Supper
described in the poem began as a joint venture in 2016.)*

My Red Dressing Gown

I sat in a pew in church in a ripped tee shirt and a bright red ladies dressing gown. Some people were leaving to go to some unknown place. I knew that I had a jumper at the back of church and that if I could put it on over my tee shirt with the missing sleeve and torn front, I would be more presentable. I stood up handed my embarrassing red dressing gown to my wife and went to get my jumper.

I heard a bang and a wardrobe door came open with a bang. I wondered what a wardrobe was doing in the middle of church so I went to investigate. The vicar came to see what the problem was and we found that a variety of clothes were piled up over six feet high and had fallen over. I realized that two shelves were missing and if the clothes were put on individual shelves the clothes would be more stable and the doors would close. Whilst we searched for the missing shelves I realised that we were in Rotherham Minster and hundreds of people from other churches were coming through the doors and I was wearing shorts a ripped tee shirt and bedroom slippers. I was embarrassed, panicked and woke up in front of my computer and the game of Solitaire that I had started had been running for over an hour. I was wearing my dressing gown but my tee shirt was not torn.
(I woke up from this dream 10 minutes before I wrote this)

The Storm

It started with a gentle breeze
Trembling leaves upon the trees
Nothing more than the hint of motion
Of rippling waves upon the ocean
Who would guess what would befall
As that gentle breeze became a squall

Who would believe it O what a sight
As the wind grew stronger in the night
What started as a gentle breeze
Blew down chimneys and uprooted trees
This mighty storm beset our nation
And left emergency services in panic stations
In October nineteen eighty seven what a sight
Fifteen million trees destroyed in one frightful night
Houses damaged, cars upended
Railways damaged, trains suspended
Our whole nation was in turmoil then.
Blaming Michael Fish on News at Ten.

Big wind, little wind were all the same back then
I go outside and fly my kite every night at half past ten
Hurricane and gentle breeze all the same to me
I once flew my kite in a nine force gale and landed in a tree
No fear I felt when a tornado struck and sucked me in the air
I grabbed my kite way up high and flew to County Clare

The people there, they honoured me as Ronald of the sky
And fed me eggs each morning and each evening apple pie
My kite to them was a symbol a treasure to them all
They put it in a special frame above the old town hall
I made kites for a living a put a deposit down
On a one way ticket on a steam train
Back to good old Rotherham Town

A New Digi Box For Ken

We've got a new Digi box to record all the programmes that we like
We're fed up watching tennis and football and a French man on his
bike
We can play our favourites on nights when there's nothing else to see
We'll never miss a show again on BBC or ITV
We've plugged in all the cables and switched the tele on
And settled down for the evening with a cup of tea and cake for Ron
We sit in anticipation for the new box to tune itself in
No signal can be found it says Oh what a mess we're in

I'll fix it in a jiffy says Ken, a new aerial lead I'll get
I've tackled much bigger problems and I've never failed you yet
An hour in the loft, my cable and electric drill I'll bring
But two hours later at twelve O'clock
He asks Celia to ring Ron for some string
I'll feed the string behind the soffit as I did fifty years ago
I'll be done by teatime easily if you really want to know
At four O' clock Ron comes round to see what progress has been
made
He's still laid down in the attic said Celia who's faith in Ken begins to
fade

Now Ken is a stalwart chap and never been known to moan
But a man with a bad back like his has been up in the loft all alone
No one will ever know in what pain martyr Ken has been
His family have put him through this agony for a better picture on the
screen
From Ron's house six houses away he can hear cries in the still night
air
Faint cries of 'whoo me back' coming from Ken's family lair
What that man must have gone through says my wife with tears in her
eyes
But knowing the high pain threshold that Ken has,
It comes to Ron as no surprise

It's now two days since we've seen him he has his meals up there you
know
He's fed seven yards of string through eaves already but none of it does
show

He comes down only to go to bed all covered in muck and spiders galore
Get washed you dirty beggar says Celia there's dirt on the bedroom floor
A good night sleep has done him good and on Sunday he's as happy as can be
He's still not fixed the problem but he's thought of a new plan B
I'll sort it out after Monday's painting group he says
Then we can have the telly on
And if my master plan fails once again, I'll blame it all on Ron

This poem is not biased towards married men not at all
For men like Ken are heroes to all men large and small
He is an example to the men in this green and pleasant land
Who are dominated by the women who have the upper hand
We will have to form a Union and get equal rights for men
Suffragettes will not be women but men like Maurice, Ron and Ken
Why is it only men who put up aerials or paint the shed bright Red
Women should do all the DIY while their men folk stay in bed

Written from a safe house by an anonymous person

The Summer Fayre

We're planning for the Summer Fayre in flaming June this year
We're raising funds for our Art Group and running out of time I fear
We're making fancy boxes for jewellery and other things
But our task will not be over till the fat lady sings
A group are making cards with cut outs and sticky stuff
Some are hand painted and we can never have enough

The craft group make shopping bags with felt animals glued around
They are all noisy workers while the art group make no sound
Maggie is making many things and her skill is beyond compare
She always has a smile for us and has flowers in her hair.
A group are making cloth dolls and animals and enjoy what they do
We'll soon have enough animals to form a fabric zoo

Some are painting pictures for sale at the Summer Fayre
You can buy our goods each Monday or wait to buy them there
We are a thirty strong Art and Craft Group
And spend over a thousand pounds each year
We raise the money at Summer and Christmas, the time of good cheer
We sometimes get a grant each year, to buy materials for each Fayre
Come along and join us we'd love to see you there

Dingle Witney Troop from Wassa Matta

On the 4th of September Last year I was happily pruning my sprouts on my side garden when a man with a leather bonnet on his head in the shape of a squirrel, popped out of the ground behind the rhubarb patch. Hello he said I'm Dingle Witney-Troop. I was amazed to see the band leader from Wassa Matta in my garden. You've ruined my Rhubarb I said but never mind it's good to see you again. I invited Dingle inside and we had tea and chocolate biscuits which my wife had hidden to prevent me from eating them when I'm on a diet. Dingle went on to say that he wanted my good friend Ken and I to come to Wassa Matta and help him find his missing band members who were needed to play at the 5,000 anniversary of the founding of Wassa Matta which was to take place in the second week in November.

We walked round to Ken's house and discovered him stuck head first in a Wendy house that he was constructing for a friend of the family. We each took a leg and pulled him out whilst Celia held on to the chimney and pulled the other way. Celia was pleased because Ken had the kettle in his hand and was in the process of making a cuppa when on a whim decided to see what the Wendy house looked like from inside. Celia's main worry was not Ken's welfare but how could she make a cup of tea without her trusty kettle which she had bought in Kettles R Us in St. Ives. Boiling water in a sauce pan would not be the same.

Over our second cup of tea in an hour Dingle explained the dilemma that he was in. After eating a couple of scones each made with double cream and lemonade, we decided to go to Wassa Matta that very evening. So using the secret entrance behind Ken's shed we entered one again into that strange and wonderful world.

We formed a posse and searched in the local area but to no avail. We set out on one of the high speed steam trains that leave the central station every twenty minutes and left the train at every station and searched the local area. Arriving at cuckoo station about three thousand miles away it was Dingle's wife Poppy Witney-Troop who found the first clue. Behind a wicket fence surrounding a large orchard she saw something reflecting the sunlight and discovered a golden trumpet which belonged to band member Horace Peabody.

On entering the orchard we discovered a spiral staircase compose entirely of willow withies. Ken was the first up the staircase and the rest of us followed. We arrived on a tropical island invisible to the people on the world above. We were met by the sound of band music. Dingle was over the moon on finding his lost band members but his mood soon changed when he realised that they were walking around in circles playing Oh I do like to be beside the seaside. Ken who had experienced this before realised that the band members had been hypnotised and never stopped playing this tune.

I looked around this small island and on a grassy mound saw the person responsible for this dilemma.
It was none other than Dilly Troop, Dingle's second cousin twice removed and owner of the golden trumpet.
We surrounded Dilly and asked for an explanation for kidnapping the entire brass band.
She reluctantly explained that she had been dropped from the band because she couldn't play the trumpet in tune with the other members and had decided that if she couldn't play with the band than no one else would hear them.

Ken asked Dilly to try and play the trumpet which he had brought with him and as she tried to play he told her to stop and he took the golden trumpet and from his man bag which was a present from Ron he produce an oil can and oiled the three piston valves and after wiping of the surplus oil with a rag, handed the trumpet back to Dilly.
The transformation was remarkable.
She joined the band in playing the tune and was note perfect

Ronald Town

The Cromford Painters in May

Now Gwen runs a workshop for painters each year
But only for those who drink red wine and beer.
In the painting room they met at ten
Ten lively ladies and three quiet men.

Paper on your boards said Gwen then I'll show you what to do
We're only using four colours today including cobalt blue
Which yellow do we need said the lady in faded jeans
No bright yellows today, we're not having any greens
But greens are good for you said one of the men
Enough of your rubbish Ron, let's start painting said Gwen

They started painting picture one with a wash on the sky
And started on another whilst, waiting for it to dry.
They painted happily did that merry bunch
And at a quarter to one went for their lunch
At the end of the day with two paintings almost done
With glasses of wine they sat in the sun.

The next day they went sketching and all had a good laugh
And sketched four buildings between four visits to the caff.
Then back to the hotel with the weather still fine
For glasses of beer and of course the red wine
Nobody knows what day three's going to bring
We've been promised no greens so maybe trees aren't the thing

Whatever the subject we know Gwen will do her best
I suspect we'll paint a sailor with a knitted string vest
Whatever we do we've enjoyed our three days
And once again this year
We've all given Gwen our whole hearted Praise.

A kitchen of Forest Green

This kitchen's a disgrace our Celia said, the worst it's ever been
Go out and buy some paint today, a lovely shade of green
Now Ken's a expert at most things and choosing paint is one
And when he arrived back home that day
His wife to her daughter's house had gone

I'll paint the kitchen said Ken and get Brownie points
And she'll think I am the best
So he covered the worktops with a sheet and put on his painting vest

He'd finished the task when Celia returned and was feeling rather glad
But instead of words of praise from her he could tell that she was mad

What were you thinking you foolish man or similar words as these
It's the wrong shade of green you've bought
And it's as thick as cottage cheese
Now Ken was surprised at this he thought it looked immense
You should have put on your glasses Ken
You've use the stuff for painting a fence

Back to the shop we'll go right now and this time you'll get it right
And after sanding the wall all next day Ken put o three coats of white
Whilst at the store Celia chose two rolls of wall paper
With a pattern of white and green
And when you've hung it to my satisfaction
The kitchen will at last look clean

Now Ken made a platform on which to stand
Made from steps and other bits
One foot on the steps and one on a stool,
Which then began to move, and Ken started to do the splits.

 He was saved that day from grief and from also looking a fool
For Celia happened to come through the door and sat upon the stool
The kitchen's now finished and looking great the best it's ever been
She proudly showed it to Ron next day
Who unwisely said why didn't you paint it green.
Now Ron has a poorly leg just now and left there without a smile
And getting away from Celia's wrath nearly ran a four minute mile

Why are My Legs so Beautiful?

Why are my legs so beautiful it's a mystery to me
And attractive to the ladies, this I cannot see
I have two swollen legs which for which there is no cure
I've been examined in hospital on the second floor
The nurses at my doctor's surgery have treated me with care
My legs hold a fascination of which I was unaware
Why are my legs so beautiful no one really knows
What is the fascination between my knees and my toes
I now wear elastic stockings from my toes up to my knee
I put them on each morning and after my cup of tea

My legs have now become famous throughout St. John's Green
From the butchers to the cake shop and other places that I've been.
Last Sunday something happened that caused me several shocks
Rumours spread throughout the church hall that Ron now wore no socks
The ladies were fascinated and asked me to show my stocking
Some though that for a man of my standing
This was something quite shocking
A lady by the name of Geraldine gave a startled shout
If my legs were so special, why was she missing out?
I went to where she was seated and now feeling quite grumpy
I cannot see what's so special she said they're short and are quite lumpy
But others disagreed with her and I'll never be the same
I'll need to seek counseling to enable me to live with all this fame
I'm now selling signed post cards of my legs with compression socks
And when people receive the through the post it will cause several shocks

The Perils of Sky Diving

A crater suddenly appeared in some sandy ground this week
And a team of experts were sent to Langar a solution for to seek
Was it a meteorite or a bomb from world war two
An earthquake or a sink hole, they hadn't got a clue
Locals heard strange screaming before the hole appeared
And thought it was an old man being strangled by his beard
Some thought they saw a grotesque shape falling from above
Could it have been superman, an eagle or even a giant dove
As the crowd looked on without making a single sound
Two sand covered heads were now seen sticking from this sandy ground
Two experts called Derek and Ron were sent for straight away
And with care and precision and JCB they cleared the sand away
People came in bus loads from that local town
As the two men from Rotherham hosed the bodies down
As the two young ladies recovered it plainly could be seen
That it was none other than Charlotte and her sister Martha Jean

They had jumped from an aeroplane to raise money for a charity of their choice

And for the first time in their lifetimes you could not hear their voice
Their dad thought it was a miracle when his daughters did not speak
And phoned the local airline and booked another jump next week
The Girls have now recovered and are talking normally once again
And Derek and Ron now wear earmuffs to try and avoid the pain.
They are now celebrities throughout our local town
But the memory that sandy hole and JCB, they'll never live it down

(It was actually a sky dive for charity)

Father's Day and Twelve Pair of Underpants

Father's Day in Yorkshire is a special time of year
When your daughter buys you chocolates
And your son buys you beer
But this year things were different for my son a meal did pay
In a posh place called the Pastures you know down Mexborough way
The meal was a carvery with turkey and Yorkshire pudding too
I had a J20 to drink and my son had a pint or two
He gave me an Amazon voucher which I spent the very next day
I liked buying thing on Amazon when I don't have to pay
I looked at art materials at books and DVDs too
At coats and shirts and jumpers just to name a few
But nothing looked just right among the things I looked at there
And then I knew just what I needed
And bought twelve pairs of underwear
When I told my wife next day
She was stunned and looked straight at me
You idiot what have you done I've just ironed you twenty three
I then jumped in quickly before she began to shout
Look on the bright side love I'm never going to run out

I went to my daughters on Father's day and pleased with this was I

For she cooked one of my favourite meals, namely cottage pie
Whilst cooking I had a pint of shandy made with real ale of course
At last dinner was ready and I could have eaten a horse
Another great meal for which I didn't have to pay
Again saving money hand over fist
And also enough veg for my six a day
And for afters I chose jam scones with cream so thick
And for my tea, whilst watching Dr Who I had a choc ice on a stick
A card and presents including money and of course chocs
And I went straight onto Amazon and ordered twelve pair of socks

The Pantry Clear Out

Clean out the pantry Ken said Celia one Friday afternoon
It's not been done for ages so you'd better do it soon
So Ken was wise as always and as cunning as a fox
And started stacking tins and stuff into a plastic box
And one box led to another as to the lounge he made another trip
And Celia watched him like a hawk and in her hand a whip

In one box he put baked beans and he counted twenty eight
These will last for ages said Ken but twenty were out of date
Fourteen tins of soup had dates of two thousand and six
How would they dispose of all this stuff they were certainly in a fix
Ken then opened a tin of mackerel which caused quite a stink
So they opened all the ancient tins and poured them down the sink

The soup went down the plug hole again and again
But so many tins of tuna, beans and prunes bunged up the drain
So Ken unscrewed the waste pipe and removed all the crap
And Celia without thinking turned on the kitchen tap
And Ken came out quickly from the cupboard door
And was covered with beans and prune juice as he lay upon the floor
They sent for Ron to help them out whilst Ken had a bath
But Ron saw the funny side and all he did was laugh
But he soon sorted out the plumbing and the kitchen floor too
But looking in the pantry saw that there was plenty more to do
They removed four bags of pasta, corn flakes and puffed wheat
Even after removing all that stuff there was still plenty to eat

After two days of intensive work the pantry was clean once more
Which was more than could be said for the prune stained kitchen floor
Why hadn't they seen that out of date stuff what was the reason why?
Celia scratched her head for a while but Ken he didn't even try
But Ken knew the reason as only our Ken could
It was hidden from his darling wife by a piece of wood

What was blocking Celia's view through that pantry door?
It had been Ken's writing slope, which had now slipped on to the floor
Now Ken had filled all the drawers with stuff and all his office too
And where to keep his writing slope he hadn't got a clue
Now Celia had cleaned out his office like many times before
And again his desk was chocka block as was his office floor

So in the pantry went his writing slope and hid the tins from view
Now Celia was angrier since when they first had wed
And Ken tripped over a plastic box and fell and banged his head
Now the pantry is immaculate with things all prim and proper
And if Ken interferes again he'll certainly come a cropper
The beans and soup are now all in code as is every other tin
And all the tins have been recycled and have filled the old black bin.

The Test Run

Now Celia has trouble walking and has fallen down again
And has to be helped from A to B by loving husband Ken
So Ken had a bright idea so he invented something new
He bought a pair of roller skates which he fastened to each shoe
He was a caring husband an knew how she would feel
So he attached a rope around her waist and on her stick he fixed a wheel

He started with a trail run one Sunday at half past six
And right at the beginning he knew he was in a fix
Celia travelled down their street waving her arms wildly about
With Ken being dragged behind on his backside and starting to shout
They turned right at the bottom past three cars and a fridge
Down thirty steps and a ramp on to the motorway bridge

Ken's trousers were getting thinner and he gradually gave up hope
Until Celia shouted loudly, Ken let go of that rope
Now Celia grabbed the rope and knew exactly what to do
She pulled the rope towards her and made a quick lasoo
A she came to the end of the bridge she hoped to soon be free
She swung the rope like a cowboy would on to the branch of a tree

Now Ken arrived at the scene bedraggled with trousers like the finest lace
To find Celia holding on to the handrail with a smile upon her face
Now Ken thought that she'd gone doolally after such an ordeal
So he put his arms around her and asked how she did feel
He expected her to be angry and feeling rather weak
But to his amazement her first words were can we do the same next week

Barry's Musical Interlude

Barry Gwyn bought a violin from the man next door
He played it sixteen hours a day until his arms were sore
Barry had some lessons from a man who owned a band
And soon became quite famous throughout our pleasant land
But Barry was quite happy in Rotherham with a stool and a hat
And made a decent living playing On Iltley Moor by tat

He played in all the local pubs a range of Christmas carols
And helped the local landlords empty many barrels
One day in an ancient pub famous for its old oak beams
He met a local cello player and the lady of his dreams
Nor Barry and Glenda were married at the beginning of the year
And instead of toasting with Champagne, they drank the local beer
They formed a quartet in the summer and played in the local bar
With Ron on his penny whistle and David on Guitar
The called themselves the Bowlers nothing to do with a cricket bat
But when playing at the local gigs the wore a bowler hat
They played folk songs like the Spinners and wrote their own stuff too
Such a dogs love balls and the Wassa Matta lullaby just to name a few

Now David was the singer of this now famous group in town
And Ron played his tin whistle all dressed in green and brown
Now Barry and Glenda dressed as a Scout and a Brownie
And played on their string instruments in the style of Mantovani
They went to local festivals and came first, third and fourth
And this summer had the honour of appearing on Look North

Thunder and lightning, wind and Snow

Memories from around Kimberworth Park from over sixty years ago

When it thundered and lightened at our house our family reacted in different ways.

We kids were excited to watch the sky lit up by the flashes and we counted the seconds between the claps of thunder which mum told us that each second counted as one mile.

My grandma Milly who lived across the road and spent much time with us was terrified and usually hid under the stairs or the table

My mother put all the cutlery away and any other metallic objects such as the kettle whilst dad switched the television off and pulled the aerial out of the socket.

Around 1959 there was an exceptionally strong gale which caused much damage nationally and during the night our chimney collapsed and came through the roof. On this occasion we were all terrified and six of under the kitchen table must have been a sight to see. The next morning I went to the Old Hall School only to find that the classrooms had been blown down. My memory is vague sixty years on but both our chimney and the school were soon repaired.

In the late sixties we seemed to have many snowy winters. One winter whilst my brother, friends and I were attending Redscope Junior school we had a deep overnight fall of snow. Snow drifts were over two feet deep and on this occasion snow had drifted to the top of the front door. Dad a miner went through the back door and cleared the snow from the front door. No buses were running and on that morning a bread van arrived outside the church. All the neighbours worked to dig a trench across the field to buy loaves from the van.

The school was open but many of the teachers who lived off the estate could not get in to work.

Much is said today about global warming and freak weather but in the past we have had our share of extreme weather conditions.

Edith

Now Edith was a real cool girl born in 1924
And was destined to be a fashion queen by the age of four
In the thirties she danced the Charleston in the latest evening gown
She wore polka dot skirts and sailor pants
In good old Rotherham Town

In the forties she was training workers about all things made of glass
Beatson Clarks were in awe of this fearsome Yorkshire lass
In the fifties she wore a swing dress and a fedora hat in brown
And all the lads knew, she was the smartest girl in town
In the sixties she wore a mini skirt and learned how to bop
She was the favourite pin up girl in the local fashion shop

In the seventies she wore a hippy skirt
And six inch platform shoes
She was the local trendsetter and always in the news
She was a radical girl and something of a shocker
She once went to the local cinema dressed as a punk rocker
In the eighties and nineties she wore a duffle coat,
To combat the winter weather

And in summer wore pleated skirts and a jacket made of leather
In the Naughties she dressed for comfort but kept her sense of style
And in her handbag kept a handkerchief, lipstick and nail file
But the strangest thing she ever wore was at the age of ninety four
And when her daughter came to visit she nearly fell on the floor
In her tenth decade she wore denim jeans all torn around the knees
She wore them in hot weather to keep cool in the summer breeze

The quiet walking group

There's was a sombre mood in the walking group In August this year
Many members walked in silence which Tony found real queer

As if raised voices bordered on being rude
Even Raymond spoke in whispers and Marian was quite subdued

When Karen shouted orders at the main road near the park
Members nearly jumped out of their skin and a dog began to bark
Conversations were carried out in whispers
And something was clearly wrong
And walking in woods near Droppingwell seemed to take so long.

Now back to the church hall they sallied and their mood was so glum
Like when kids are told its bedtime and are unhappy with their mum
During refreshments things were no better
And seeing Ron didn't change their mood
And when he asked what was the matter
They thought he was being quite rude.

The following week things were back to normal with that gallant crowd
And once again voices were heard and one voice was especially loud
It was Karen who solved the problem why something was amiss
Last week a dozen chocolate biscuits left the group were missing Chris.

My Working Life

I started work as a joiner after leaving school
And bought a brace and bit. A mashing can and a three foot rule
And with a joiners plane and a variety of tools
I worked on pubs and houses and also local schools

I learned my trade from Colin, Frank, Reg and Bill
How to fit a door, a roof and a window cill
How to make a window frame a staircase and a door.
How to level floor joists and how to fix a floor

I studied at college with Albert, Doug and Fred
And at twenty seven years I was finally wed
I loved all my years working with all types of wood
I perfected my skill and my life it has been good
I did my job as best as I was able
Because I was also a carpenter born in a stable. ***
I started teaching joinery at the age of thirty two
To apprentices from the building works and steel works just to name a few

I showed them how to do the things that I had been shown myself
To fixing rafters on a roof to a fixing a humble shelf
I taught theory and science and also geometry and maths
I had many enjoyable lessons and also many laughs

In the workshop we began our lesson by sharpening all our tools
Most students were brilliant with the occasional set of fools
I felt proud as their skills developed and they became quite adept
I remember many things they made and the memories I have kept

But the most rewarding time was easy enough to guess
When a student passed their exams and were overjoyed at their success

*** (I was actually born in Moorgate Hospital but we lived in Aldwarke Cottages
Which were converted stables built by Lord and Lady Egerton who live at Aldwarke Hall.
My Grandfather George was groom and coachman there in the early twentieth century)*

Twelve Sheds From My Window

I look out of my bedroom window when I get out of bed
And every garden I can see has at least one shed
Some are old and some are new and some are fantastic
Most of them are made of wood and one is made of plastic

Of the twelve variety of sheds that I can see
You may not believe me if I say that I myself have built three
Two I built by myself but I can't remember when
But the best of all was a summerhouse I built with my good friend Ken

This shed was almost doomed from the start and left us both forlorn
I carried plywood up a slope and fell backwards on the lawn
Not to be outdone Ken fell off his steps
And on his backside he did land
And I almost fainted at the sight of Ken with blood upon his hand

I rushed Ken down to the house thinking things could not get worse
But medical treatment was swiftly given by his daughter who is a nurse
Other mishaps we did have but we both enjoyed the task
If you want to know to do the same you only need to ask

Now sadly no more sheds for us to build
For we have both done our bit
And leave the job to other men who are younger and are also fit.
We finished the shed after many weeks and it certainly did look grand
We launched it on a summer's day with glass of wine,

A piece of cake and to a CD of a brass band.

*(I wrote this after reading a small book called **The Specialist** by **Charles Sale.**
It tells the story of an American specialist early last century who builds wooden privies and tells how
he looks and admires them from the road above whilst eating his dinner)*

(View from my bedroom window)

Ties and Jumpers

I bought a tie from Marks and Sparks in nineteen sixty four
It cost me all of two and six and not a penny more
The tie was called a Tootal tie and all the rage back then
I wore it on many occasions until the year twenty ten
The tie is now in tatters and the colours have begun to fade
I keep it as a tribute to the best tie ever made

I had a collection of other ties of every colour and style
I wore a tie of a shade of red when I walked down the aisle
In the sixties and seventies and that's a long way back
I wore a white tie from John Speeds and a shirt of colour black
Ties were the height of fashion for all way back then
And were worn on every occasion by all the local men

I no longer wear ties for work as I used to do
Jumpers are my new true love and I have thirty two
I wear them on every occasion and they match my shirt and hat
Some are smooth and silky and some as hairy as a cat
Some were bought a Sweater Shop and are known as retro today

I bought them in the eighties and five pounds had to pay

Tootal ties on Ebay are twenty pound or more
And Sweater Shop jumpers now cost thirty four
All my jumpers and my ties were all top of the pops
But you can still pick them up if you're lucky in several charity shops
Being the height of fashion is no longer important to me
I'm happy if things are warm ad fit me as I approach seventy three

(Even fifteen year old college students wore a shirt and tie in the 1960's and baseball caps were unknown)

Shunned by All

Why do people in the walking group ignore me,
I'm beginning to wonder why
Is it because I'm invisible or because I'm extremely shy?
I've become a non entity someone who does not exist
Or have I been sent to Coventry or on an national avoidance list

Or is it my new hobbies
Like collecting train numbers and breeding Yorkshire skunks
Or juggling with coconuts whilst eating pineapple chunks
Or spending my days writing poems and planing lumps of wood
Or because every Wednesday I wear green clothing
And pretend to be Robin Hood

I'm suddenly an outcast and always, excluded and on my own
Spending time checking for non existent Emails
On my new smart phone
I suddenly know the reason and realised that I'll never be the same
Because I haven't walked for a year and a half,
They've all forgotten my name

Now I'm out of my depression, it's like I'm newly born
Maggie made me a bacon butty and smiled at me last Friday morn
Things are now looking rosier people are talking to me again
You know I don't hold grudges, so don't forget my name.

Painting by the author

Printed in Great Britain
by Amazon

84768271R00129